CONSTANTINE V. PRINCE

Second Edition

Constantine v. Prince

Second Edition

William Bailey

Professor from Practice
University of Washington School of Law

NATIONAL INSTITUTE FOR TRIAL ADVOCACY

Address inquiries to:
Reprint Permission
National Institute for Trial Advocacy
1685 38th Street, Suite 200
Boulder, CO 80301-2735
Phone: (800) 225-6482
Fax: (720) 890-7069
E-mail: permissions@nita.org

ISBN 978-1-60156-292-0
FBA 1292

CONTENTS

ACKNOWLEDGMENTS

The author gratefully acknowledges the help and encouragement of Jeanne Philotoff of NITA and Anthony J. Bocchino of Temple University Beasley School of Law, without whom this case file never would have happened; the insight and strategic analysis of Professor Emeritus Frederick Moss of Southern Methodist University, whose thoughtful input was a great help in identifying improvements needed in this edition; the professionalism and expertise of Detective Kevin Andrews of the Traffic Fatality Investigation Unit of the Seattle Police Department; the creative talent of computer animator Jay Syverson of OnPoint Productions, Seattle, Washington, and illustrator Duane Hoffmann of Hoffmann Legal Design, Seattle, Washington; and most importantly, the Philippides family, whose strength of character and devotion to one another will always be an inspiration. Their son and brother Yianni was taken from them far too soon. Though a young man at the time of his death, he was a wise old soul whose philosophy of life continues to have meaning for me.

INTRODUCTION

This is a wrongful death case involving a bicyclist who was hit in the crosswalk by a motorist. The decedent's estate seeks to recover damages from the defendant, alleging that he was negligent in going too fast, sending a text message while driving, and not keeping a proper lookout for decedent. The defendant denies the plaintiff's claims of negligence and asserts that the decedent's death was caused by his own contributory negligence.

The plaintiff's estate claims that he would have gone on to law school and earned income consistent with those with graduate degrees. The defendant denies this, countering that decedent had not actually yet earned a college degree and had failed to take any tangible steps toward becoming a lawyer. He had worked for several years as a bicycle messenger without any indication that he intended to return to school, let alone to go to law school. The defendant cites the plaintiff's use of marijuana; body tattoos; and alternative, non-materialistic philosophy of life as further proof that he was unlikely to become a lawyer.

An essential component of the defendant's contributory negligence claim is that the decedent was not wearing a bicycle helmet. There is conflicting evidence on this point. The other main defense liability argument is that the defendant's approaching SUV was visible to the decedent and should have caused him to remain on the corner rather than enter the crosswalk. The defendant further states that his view of the crosswalk was blocked by cars in the right turn lane.

The defense also has a factual argument that the decedent bicycle messenger, who was killed at the end of his work day, had rush deliveries he had to make, but without enough time to do them.

The defendant crossed out part of the statement he gave to the police at the scene and refused to sign it, raising the question of impeachment.

Computer animations are used by the accident reconstruction experts on each side, supporting their respective liability theories.

The laws of the State of Nita govern the trial of this case. There is no issue of jurisdiction, venue, service of process, propriety of the parties, or question that the defendant was in the scope and course of employment at the time of the collision. The applicable laws are contained in the proposed jury instructions that are set forth at the end of the case file.

Pleadings

IN THE CIRCUIT COURT OF
DARROW COUNTY, NITA
CIVIL DIVISION

MELINA CONSTANTINE, as	)	
Personal Representative of	)	CIVIL ACTION
the Estate of GEORGE	)	CA 02-013
CONSTANTINE,	)	
	)	
Plaintiff,	)	
	)	
v.	)	
	)	
RICHARD PRINCE,	)	
	)	
Defendant.	)	
	)	

COMPLAINT

COMES NOW the Plaintiff and makes an amended claim for damages against defendant, stating in the following particulars:

I. PARTIES AND JURISDICTION

1.1 Plaintiff Melina Constantine is the surviving sister of, and the personal representative of, the Estate of George Constantine.

1.2 At all times material hereto, defendant Richard Prince resided at 259 Lewiston Road, Minneapolis, Minnesota.

1.3 On or about June 22, 2012, defendant Richard Prince was operating a motor vehicle on the public highways of Darrow County.

1.4 At all times material, defendant Richard Prince was an employee of Worldwide Footwear, Inc., and was acting within the course and scope of that employment.

II. LIABILITY

2.1 On or about June 22, 2012, at approximately 4:50 p.m., George Constantine was operating a bicycle westbound in the crosswalk at the intersection of Sunset Street and Empire Way in Nita, Darrow County.

2.2 Defendant Richard Prince was proceeding northbound on Empire Way. Defendant Richard Prince was negligent, and his negligence proximately caused the collision that inflicted severe and fatal injuries on George Constantine, including blunt force trauma to the head.

Plaintiff realleges the statements contained in Paragraphs 2.1 and 2.2

2.3   At all times material, defendant Richard Prince was employed by and driving a vehicle rented by Worldwide Footwear, Inc., and, at the time of the facts alleged herein, was acting within the course and scope of that employment.

III.   INJURIES AND DEATH

3.1   As a direct and proximate result of the negligence of defendant, George Constantine suffered severe injuries. He clung to life in a comatose condition for seven days, and he then died at Memorial Hospital in Nita, Darrow County, on June 29, 2012, as a result of the injuries negligently inflicted upon him.

IV.   DAMAGES

4.1   As a direct and proximate result of the negligence of defendant, the Estate of George Constantine incurred medical expenses, funeral expenses, lost wages, and loss of earning capacity.

4.2   As a further result of said defendant's negligence, The Estate of George Constantine is entitled to compensation for the pain, anguish, disability, and loss of enjoyment of life suffered by George Constantine.

V.   PRAYER FOR RELIEF

WHEREFORE, plaintiff prays for judgment against defendant for damages in a reasonable sum to be proved at trial, taxable costs of this action, attorney's fees, and further relief as seems just and proper.

DATED this 28th day of July, 2012.

SCHERER & GILLIG

Andrew C. Scherer

ANDREW C. SCHERER

Attorney at Law
Nita Professional Center

IN THE CIRCUIT COURT OF
DARROW COUNTY, NITA
CIVIL DIVISION

MELINA CONSTANTINE, as Personal Representative of the Estate of GEORGE CONSTANTINE, Plaintiff, v. RICHARD PRINCE, Defendant.	))))))))))))))	CIVIL ACTION CA 02-013

ANSWER

Defendant Richard Prince, for his answer to plaintiff's Complaint for Personal Injuries, hereby admit, deny, and allege as follows:

1. Answering paragraph 1.1, defendant is without sufficient information to admit or deny the allegations contained therein and, therefore, denies same.

2. Answering paragraph 1.2, defendant admits the allegations contained therein.

3. Answering paragraph 1.3, defendant admits the allegations contained therein.

4. Answering paragraph 1.4, defendant admits the allegations contained therein.

5. Answering paragraph 2.1, defendant admits that George Constantine was operating a bicycle. Defendant is without sufficient information to admit or deny the remaining allegations in paragraph 2.1 and, therefore, denies same.

6. Answering paragraph 2.2, defendant admits that Richard Prince was proceeding northbound on Empire Way. Defendant denies the remaining allegations in paragraph 2.2.

   Defendant realleges his responses to the statements contained in paragraphs 2.1 and 2.2 as if fully set forth herein.

7. Answering paragraph 2.3, defendant admits the allegations contained therein.

8. Answering paragraph 3.1, defendant admits that George Constantine died at Memorial Hospital in Nita, Darrow County on June 29, 2012. Defendant further admits that George Constantine suffered severe injuries. Defendant denies the remaining allegations in paragraph 3.1.

9. Answering paragraph 4.1, defendant denies the allegations contained therein.

10. Answering paragraph 4.2, defendant denies the allegations contained therein.

AFFIRMATIVE DEFENSE

1. Plaintiff's damages may have been caused in whole or in part by the conduct of George Constantine and any damages must be reduced accordingly.

2. Plaintiff's complaint fails to state a claim upon which relief can be granted.

3. Defendant reserves the right to assert additional affirmative defenses as further discovery may warrant.

WHEREFORE, having answered Plaintiff's Complaint for Personal Injuries, defendant prays for the following relief:

1. That plaintiff's complaint be dismissed with prejudice.

2. For the award of reasonable attorneys' fees and costs, as allowed under the applicable court rules and statutes; and

3. For such other and further relief as this Court may deem equitable and just.

DATE: October 29, 2012

BRIGATI, COLOMBO & HAWKS, PS

By *Teresa Brigati*

Teresa Brigati

Attorney for Defendant

INVESTIGATION DOCUMENTS

TRANSCRIBED STATEMENT OF WITNESS

DATE: June 22, 2012

TIME: 1830 hours

PLACE: 1100 Block, Empire Way

NAME: Paul Burley

DOB: 1/10/82

On June 22, 2012, at approximately 1650 hours, I was driving S/B in the 1100 block of Empire Way. I am a truck driver for Swifty Auto Parts and was headed to the south end for a delivery to one of our stores.

As I slowed down approaching the intersection, I saw a bicyclist approaching the N/E corner of the intersection. He was pedaling very slowly and looking for traffic. I scanned the area as I came to a stop.

All of a sudden, I heard a collision. I looked to my left and saw the bicyclist on the hood of the dark-colored SUV.

Paul Burley

Paul Burley

Leo Carillo

Witness, Officer Leo Carillo
Statement taken by
Officer Leo Carillo
Nita Police Department
Serial No. 6003, Unit 413

TRANSCRIBED STATEMENT OF WITNESS

DATE: June 22, 2012

TIME: 1800 hours

PLACE: 1100 Block, Empire Way

NAME: Curtis Parsons

DOB: 9/28/77

On June 22, 2012, at approximately 1650 hours, I was waiting to make a left turn onto Sunset Street from S/B Empire Way. I was stopped for traffic in the inside lane, and there were no other cars in front of me. This is an uncontrolled intersection with no traffic light or pedestrian walk signals.

While I waited for the N/B traffic to clear, I saw a bicyclist waiting at the crosswalk on the N/E corner of the intersection. He was stopped as he watched N/B traffic pass in front of him.

When there was a break in the oncoming traffic, I saw the bicyclist prepare to cross the street on his bike. We made eye contact. In that I was going to wait for him to cross in front of me before I made my turn, I motioned with my hand to wave him across the street. After this, the bicyclist started out into the street, pedaling slowly.

The bicyclist was struck in the crosswalk by a dark-colored SUV, which was N/B in the inside lane. It came out of nowhere. I hadn't seen the vehicle until an instant before the collision with the bicycle. My attention was somewhat divided as there was a great deal of car and pedestrian traffic. When I had last seen him, before the impact, the bicyclist had just pushed off with his foot and was beginning to pedal W/B in the crosswalk across Empire Way.

Curtis Parsons

Curtis Parsons

Leo Carillo

Witness, Officer Leo Carillo
Statement taken by
Officer Leo Carillo
Nita Police Department
Serial No. 6003, Unit 413

NITA POLICE DEPARTMENT
TRAFFIC DEPARTMENT FATALITY INVESTIGATION

Incident No.:   8855251

Principal Investigator: Detective Robin S. Cruise, Nita Police Department

I arrived on the scene of the accident on June 22, 2012, at approximately 1800 hours. I assigned Officers Richard Sears and Leo Carillo to taking witness statements. The bicyclist, George Constantine, had been taken by Nita Fire Department paramedics to Memorial Hospital. I talked to the driver of the SUV, Richard Prince, prior to Officer Sears taking a statement from him. He told me that he had not seen the bicyclist until he heard the sound of his vehicle making contact with him, due to cars in the right turn lane blocking his view of the intersection.

This investigator conducted an examination of the SUV at the scene. The primary area of impact was on the hood above the right headlight assembly. There was a large trough-shaped depression along the leading edge and surface of the hood. The depression was angled. This was likely the result of contact between the bicyclist's left leg and the vehicle's hood. The shape and contour of the depression mirrored the shape and flex position of the bicyclist's left leg. There was a fabric smear on the hood surface resulting from contact with the bicyclist's clothing. The windshield glass was also damaged in the impact. There were two impact areas. The damage resulted from the bicyclist's head and left shoulder striking the windshield.

I examined the interior of the vehicle. It was equipped with an automatic transmission. The gear selector was in the "P" or "Park" position. The emergency brake was engaged. The ignition was switched "Off." When this investigator switched the ignition "On," the radio was on, tuned to the Fred Rabble talk show. The air conditioning was set on maximum. The fan for this unit was set in the "Medium" position. There were glass shards from the damaged windshield spread throughout the interior of the vehicle. The brake and gas pedal pads showed signs of minimal wear. A cellular telephone, map, and daytime planning book lay on the right front passenger seat. The odometer read 1416 miles. The vehicle was equipped with a power-assisted, four-wheel Anti-Lock Braking System (ABS).

After observing the cellular telephone, I questioned the driver about what use he might have been making of it prior to the collision. While he denied any such use, his demeanor and facial mannerisms were nervous, leading me strongly to suspect that he was not telling me the truth. At this point, I gave him his *Miranda* rights and asked if he would continue to answer questions about the incident. He said that he "had nothing to hide" and would answer any and all questions. I asked the driver if I could examine the phone, and he readily agreed, saying "I have nothing to hide. This was an accident, it was not my fault."

On examining the phone, I saw the following partially completed text message on the screen: "Want to get home. Really tired. Trying to change my flight. . . ." At this point, I said to the driver, "Tell me the truth. Were you texting prior to the collision?" He admitted it generally, but denied doing so in the moments before the accident: "I had done it earlier while headed north on Empire Way, but stopped after the traffic got too bad. I was scared that you wouldn't believe me, so I didn't tell you the truth at first."

I cannot remember whether I saw a helmet at the scene or not. One of our photos has an object on the road near the victim's body that may be a helmet. I cannot tell from the photo.

Witness Parsons saw the bicyclist waiting at the northeast corner of the intersection of Empire Way and Sunset Streets. He noticed there was a break in the heavy volume of N/B traffic. He made eye contact with the bicyclist and then decided to wait until the bicyclist crossed Empire Way W/B in front of his stopped vehicle. Parsons saw the bicyclist push off with his foot and start to cross. He did not see Prince's SUV until an instant before it struck the bicyclist. Parsons emphasized to me the suddenness of the SUV's appearance by stating, "It came out of nowhere. He had to be going fast."

I then talked to witness Burley, who also saw the bicyclist waiting at the N/E corner of the intersection. He saw the bicyclist pedaling as he approached the corner from the east.

The driver and witness statements focus the issues that I concerned myself with in this investigation: perception/reaction, speed, conspicuity, time/distance, and driver behavior prior to, at, and after impact. The subjective speed estimate for the SUV prior to impact ranged from the driver's estimate of 20–25 mph to Parsons nonspecific estimate that the SUV was "really flying."

To come up with an objective range of pre-impact speeds for the SUV, I considered the following data:

1. The roadway's adjusted coefficient of friction, as measured by our drag sled. The SUV was equipped with ABS. The roadway surface was new Portland cement with grooves perpendicular to traffic flow direction. No mechanical problems were noted with the vehicle's braking system. It was new, with low mileage (1416 miles traveled).

2. The distance between the area of the impact and the SUV's place of rest was approximately eighty-five feet. Several small scrapes were located in the roadway surface of the crosswalk. These were of recent origin. Their appearance was consistent with other bicycle-caused scrapes observed by this investigator. The location of the scrapes was consistent with witness Parson's statement, which provided independent support for placing the bicyclist in the north crosswalk of the intersection prior to impact.

3. The damage pattern to the SUV's hood provided a critical clue to the pre-impact position of the bicyclist's leg. The dent displacement to the hood described the outline of the bicyclist's left leg from approximately mid-shin area to the left hip. The damage pattern indicates the bicyclist's left leg was in a relatively high position.

4. The damage pattern to the SUV's hood also provided a critical clue to the location of the bicyclist's center of gravity at the impact. It was located either at the same height or even slightly above the height of the leading edge of the SUV's hood.

5. Pre-impact braking by the SUV would cause the front end of the vehicle to dip. The lowered front end would then ramp the bicyclist onto the vehicle. Pre-impact braking would result in a longer ride time by the bicyclist and drop off in front of the vehicle. The damage to the vehicle, the path of the bicyclist's body, and the final position of the bicycle on the

pavement in front of the stopped SUV lead me to believe that the driver applied his brakes prior to impact.

6. The bicyclist in this accident was riding a custom-built high performance bicycle. He was a young man in good physical condition. To come up with a speed for the bicyclist from the corner of the intersection where he started to the place where he was struck, I performed tests using a former nationally ranked competitive bicyclist. The rider was balanced on the bicycle and stopped without his feet touching the ground. The rider's feet were clipped into the bicycle pedals. The pedal positions approximated clock positions of three and nine o'clock. Nine timed sample rides were conducted over a fixed distance of twenty feet. The observed times ranged from 1.7–2.5 seconds. The times, acceleration rates, and acceleration factor were all higher than comparable fast tests in published academic studies. The acceleration rate for the bicyclist was calculated using the slowest time of 2.5 seconds.

7. This investigator conducted a series of braking tests on August 17, 2012. A Ford Crown Victoria equipped with ABS was used as the test vehicle. Four ranges of speed were used—20, 30, 40, and 50 mph. Three test runs each were performed at speeds of 20, 30, and 40 mph. The test proved that the vehicle had sufficient area to stop when braking occurred at the identified area of impact.

CONCLUSIONS

Based on all the tests and calculations by this investigator, I was able to come to the following conclusions:

1. The low end of the speed range for the SUV was estimated at approximately 26 mph. The high end of the speed range was estimated at approximately 36 mph. Given that there was a volume of vehicle and pedestrian traffic at the time of the collision, it is possible that the SUV was going the low end of the speed range. The traffic volumes in the immediate area of the accident, as well as in the surrounding blocks, would not easily accommodate a vehicle traveling at speeds in excess of this.

   The driver of the SUV said he was blocked or trapped in the northbound lane by the volume of traffic. This is consistent with traffic conditions in this area at the time of the accident. South of this roadway expansion point, traffic flow tends to be slow. Vehicles move at speeds slower than the unposted arterial speed of 30 mph.

2. However, the impact damage to the SUV was more consistent with a speed at the high end of the speed range. There was greater consistency in the data when I presumed pre-impact braking by Mr. Prince. Though he claimed not to have braked until he heard the impact, I believe he undoubtedly did so prior to that time. This sequence of events happened so fast, he just didn't realize this.

3. The driver probably had sufficient time/distance to avoid this accident. At a speed of 25 mph, the SUV would travel approximately fifty-five feet at a constant rate of speed. The SUV would then need approximately twenty-five feet to come to a stop at this speed. At 36 mph, the SUV would travel approximately seventy-nine feet at a constant rate of speed. The SUV

would then need approximately fifty feet to come to a stop. The distance between the south and north edges of the intersection was approximately forty-five feet. During the on-scene investigation, the north crosswalk was visible approximately fifty feet south of the southern edge of the intersection. The accident occurred during daylight hours. Lighting was not a factor.

Robin Cruise

Detective Robin Cruise
Investigation Officer
Nita Police Department
Serial No. 5377, Unit 761

TRANSCRIBED STATEMENT OF WITNESS

DATE: June 22, 2012

TIME: 1753 hours

PLACE: 1100 Block, Empire Way

NAME: Prince, Richard E.

DOB: 7/28/74

My name is Richard Prince. On June 22, at approximately 5:00 p.m., I was driving on Empire Way. Traffic wasn't stop-and-go, but it was busy. Really, the first time I saw the bicyclist, I didn't really see him. I heard it first. It happened so fast. The first time I saw him, he was on the hood. Actually, right on the windshield. Cars in the right turn lane had blocked my view of the bicyclist as I approached the intersection.

When I realized I had hit the bicyclist, I braked. I was in the lefthand lane of northbound traffic. It was such a surprise, I didn't realize what had happened. I immediately braked, and he rolled off the hood. I knew there was an impact, but I didn't know what it was. The impact, I imagine, I don't really know where it happened.

Besides the cars in the lane to the right of me, there was rush hour traffic all around me. I braked and brought the SUV to a stop. I jumped out and tried to establish the extent of the bicyclist's injuries and the damage to my rental car.

I was coming from the Indulgence Tower Hotel. I was driving north on Empire Way. I stayed in the lane closest to the center line. I would guess that I was going around 20 mph. Probably 20–25 mph. I was on Empire Way looking for a place to have dinner.

_____

(Refused) Statement taken by Officer R. Sears

R. Sears

Witness, Officer R. Sears
Serial No. 5655, Unit 412
Nita Police Department

DARROW COUNTY MEDICAL EXAMINER'S OFFICE
MEDICAL EXAMINER'S RECORD

Case No.:	236-1239
Date Reported:	June 29, 2012
Time:	1937 Hours
Last Name:	Constantine
First Name:	George
Date of Death:	June 29, 2012
Sex:	M
Race:	Caucasian
Age:	22
City, Town, or Location of Death:	Nita
In City Limits?:	Yes
Resident's Street	
Address:	805 West Blaine
City:	Nita
County:	Darrow
Incident Street Address:	Empire Way & Sunset City, Nita
Occupation at	
Time of Death:	Bike messenger
Hospital Name:	Memorial

CIRCUMSTANCES OF DEATH

The case was reported by Memorial Hospital as the death of a man, status post-traumatic injuries. The decedent is reported to have been involved in a car versus bicycle collision at Empire Way and Sunset Streets in downtown Nita. Mr. Constantine was admitted to Memorial Hospital at approximately 1845 hours on June 22, 2012, having been transported to the emergency department by a Medic 10. Mr. Constantine was treated at Memorial Hospital until his death at 1858 hours on June 29, 2012.

The following is from Nita police reportage. Mr. Constantine is reported to have been attempting to cross Empire Way in a marked crosswalk on his bicycle when he is said to have been struck by an SUV. The roadway is reported to have been dry and the weather clear. Mr. Constantine is reported to have not been wearing a helmet. At this writing, the Nita Police Department's investigation and accident reconstruction is ongoing.

PATHOLOGICAL DIAGNOSIS

1. Blunt force injury to the head with:

    a. Subgaleal hemorrhage.

    b. Status post-craniectomy.

    c. Right calvarial skull fracture (at craniectomy site).

    d. Multiple cerebral contusions, right and left in base of brain.

    e. Large intraparenchymal hemorrhage, right, deep white matter in basal ganglia.

2. Blunt force injury to the trunk and extremities with subcutaneous abrasions and contusions.

3. Acute bronchopneumonia.

OPINION

The cause of death in this twenty-two-year-old man was multiple cerebral hemorrhage due to blunt force trauma to the head. Contributing to his death is acute bronchopneumonia, which developed during the course of his hospitalization. Given the circumstances and autopsy findings, the manner of death is accident (traffic).

Judith I. Dunglison

Judith I. Dunglison
Associate Medical Examiner
Date Signed: July 30, 2012

EXTERNAL EXAMINATION

Identification is accomplished by name tags accompanying the body. In addition, photographs were taken under my direction for identification purposes. There is no clothing on or accompanying the body.

The body is that of a normally developed, well-nourished male who appears his recorded age of twenty-two years, weighs 188 pounds, and measures 6'3" in height. The body is cold to the touch. Rigor mortis is four plus in the extremities and jaw. The body is well preserved and not embalmed.

The scalp is covered by short dark brown hair measuring up to one-quarter inch. There is evidence of medical therapy, which will be described in greater detail below.

Identifying marks: On the back of the calves of both the right and left legs is a dark-colored tattoo. On the right leg the tattoo consists of a figure that appears to be "Kokopelli." On the back of the left calf is a circular design.

EXTERNAL EVIDENCE OF THERAPY

There is a craniectomy incision in the scalp and extends from the left frontal scalp posterior to the mid-posterial parietal scalp for eight inches. These margins are approximated with surgical sutures and the margins are unremarkable.

There are needle puncture marks in the right clavicular region, antecubital fossae, and right inguinal region.

On the left collateral chest is a medical incision, which has a single suture approximating the margins. This is most consistent with a previous chest tube.

EXTERNAL EVIDENCE OF INJURY

1. There are bilateral faint purple-red contusions of the periorbital tissue of both eyes. There is yellow discoloration on the periphery. On the right side of the face there are also scattered abrasions.

2. On the right anterior knee is a healing red-brown abrasion measuring one-half inch with overlying granulation tissue.

3. On the right posterior elbow is a healing one-and-one-quarter-inch abrasion.

4. On the left elbow is a healing abrasion measuring three-quarter of an inch with surrounding early scar formation.

5. On the left lateral iliac region extending slightly onto the back is a red-brown contusion which measures 3×3 inches.

6. On the left lateral knee region is a healing yellow-red abrasion measuring 2×2 inches.

INTERNAL EVIDENCE OF INJURY

1. The scalp is reflected and shows the diffuse subgaleal hemorrhage, most prominent over the right hemisphere.

2. There is a previous craniectomy.

3. There is diffuse cerebral edema.

4. There are multiple cerebral contusions seen externally on the right superior sagittal region near the central sulcus and show a focal contusion.

5. Externally there is evidence of fungus cerebri of the right lateral hemisphere and measures 5×4 inches. This corresponds to the above-described craniectomy.

ORGAN SYSTEMS

There is no gross hypertrophy of the heart. The coronary arteries are normally disposed. The respiratory system shows no abnormalities. The gastrointestinal and urinary systems are unremarkable. As previously noted, the brain shows evidence of acute hemorrhage.

DEATH INVESTIGATION TOXICOLOGY REPORT

Screen for ethanol—negative. Urine test results not performed. Drug screen cannabinoids—negative.

Report of Questioned Document Examiner, Bernard H. Friedman

I am a trained, certified examiner of questioned documents with twenty-five years of experience in law enforcement who has spent the last five years working as a consultant in legal cases following my retirement from the FBI.

After receiving a BS degree in Criminal Justice from Southern Illinois University, I received my law degree from Indiana University. Thereafter, I was hired by the FBI, where I was trained as a specialist in the examination of questioned documents, receiving both the basic and the advanced certification in this field at the FBI Academy.

Over the course of my career in law enforcement, I have studied thousands of documents in criminal cases and have testified in many trials. I have served in many civil cases as a document expert since shifting my career emphasis as a self-employed consultant.

I was retained by counsel for the plaintiff in the case to examine the handwritten statement of defendant Richard Prince that was taken from him at the scene by Office Sears on June 22, 2012. Several statements had been crossed out. My assignment was to determine the content of these.

However, a questioned document examiner never can be an advocate for any side. Rather, it is our purpose to apply our expertise in a neutral fashion, assisting the court, not a particular side. This is exactly the way I was trained by the FBI, and I apply this training to all the cases in which I have been involved.

At my request, plaintiff's counsel made a motion to the court to get the original statement from the police file for me to analyze, as it would not be possible for me to do my examination with a photocopy. The judge ordered this to be done. Thereafter, I went to police headquarters, where the records custodian provided the original document to me.

Infrared imaging equipment and photography are valuable tools for document examiners like myself in situations like this. There is much more of the light spectrum than the human eye can see. For example, when we look at a rainbow, we cannot see either the infrared (IR) or ultraviolet (UV) light.

The instruments we need to convert the IR and UV components into visible images are called video-spectral comparators and forensic imaging spectrometers. This equipment is used for the nondestructive analysis of questioned documents, such as the handwritten statement of the defendant in this case.

With IR and UV light, we can see "through" writing that has been blacked out or covered up by "white out," as well as scribbled out writing such as we have here. Under an IR filter, the scribbled out writing on the handwritten statement was visible as a luminescence.

Following my examination of the handwritten statement with the equipment I have described, I made a copy of the luminescent words that appeared under the layer of ink scribbled on top. The following two statements had been crossed out: "I thought a rock hit the windshield" and "There was traffic to the right side."

Defendant's Statement

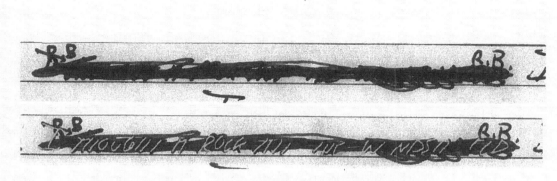

I thought a rock hit the windshield

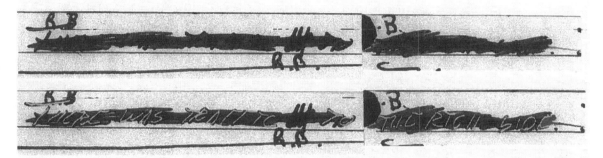

There was traffic to the right side.

DEPOSITIONS

Deposition of Melina Constantine
April 5, 2013

1   My name is Melina Constantine. I am a twenty-eight-year-old attorney. George Constantine
2   was my younger brother. I work for the Plimpton, Standish firm in downtown Nita.
3
4   I graduated from law school in May of 2012, only a few weeks before my brother was killed.
5   I had previously worked for the Plimpton, Standish firm in marketing. I wrote brochures and
6   press releases and did client relation assignments.
7
8   I was the oldest of three in my family. Next came my brother Demetrious, who is an engineer,
9   and then George.
10
11 My father was born in Athens, Greece, and lived there until he was almost forty. That's when
12 he married my mom. He was in the United States doing graduate work at the University of
13 Nita. He met my mom on a blind date. They were married the following year.
14
15 My father grew up in hard times. He married my mother later in life, after establishing himself
16 as a respected and well-paid airline pilot. After he had children of his own, he did not want
17 them to be exposed to the kind of turmoil he had experienced growing up. Unstable political
18 and economic conditions in Greece caused my parents to decide that it would be best to raise
19 their family in the United States. That's when my family came to this country, moving to an
20 agricultural area in rural Darrow County.
21
22 My father is the demanding quiet one, and my mother is the talkative nurturer. She was
23 the kind of stay-at-home mom who would make fresh bread and cookies, drive us to all our
24 activities, help us with whatever we needed. I felt that my brothers and I had a good life, but
25 I didn't realize then just how lucky we were.
26
27 There was six years' difference between George and I, so we really didn't develop a close
28 relationship until he moved to Nita and started college. It's funny, six years is a lot when
29 you're ten and sixteen, but not so much when you are eighteen and twenty-four.
30
31 George was always a happy little kid. He was a good artist and into reading. His teachers
32 always remarked that he was exceptionally bright. He was also a risk taker, someone who
33 would get in trouble for speaking out in class.
34
35 We traveled very often as a family, particularly in the summer. We would go back to visit my
36 father's sister and her family, who are still in Athens. Our parents also wanted us to get an idea
37 of what the United States was about, so we would go to national parks during the summer.

1   My parents kept a number of Greek customs, which were a part of our growing up. Easter is a
2   big holiday in Greece, and there is a tradition that's supposed to be good luck when you dye
3   Easter eggs bright red. If you tap it on the person next to you and the egg doesn't crack, you're
4   supposed to have good luck for the upcoming year. On New Year's Eve, we'd all pile into the
5   car to leave home to take a short trip. This was also part of the Greek tradition. When you
6   came home, you'd throw a pomegranate on the driveway before you entered the home, and
7   that's supposed to bring luck, prosperity, and safety for the family.
8
9   Our parents have always been strong about the importance of family. They told all of us that
10   no matter what you do, your family will always accept you. In the end, you always have your
11   family for whatever support you need.
12
13   When we first moved to the United States, my parents didn't have furniture in a couple of
14   rooms for years. They were saving money to help us so we wouldn't have to work and go to
15   college at the same time. My parents sacrificed quite a bit for us. But I think if you ask them,
16   they wouldn't say it was a sacrifice at all. It was something that they believed in, something
17   that gave them joy.
18
19   George visited me a few times at the University of Nita while he was in high school. When
20   he came to the university, we developed a more adult-like relationship. We traveled through
21   Europe together one summer. He taught me how to snowboard.
22
23   After I had graduated from University of Nita and began to work at the Plimpton, Standish
24   firm in marketing, my brother would ask me about my job. When I began law school, he began
25   to ask me questions about that as well. By this point, he had left the University of Nita and was
26   working as a bicycle messenger. My parents had very high expectations for us in terms of our
27   schoolwork. My brother graduated from high school early and was doing college-level work
28   during his senior year. Four years later, he told our parents that he wanted to take a year or
29   two off for "playtime" and then get serious about his future.
30
31   He had embraced Eastern religious thought in college. He hung out with an alternative
32   crowd—intellectuals and free spirits. He smoked marijuana on a regular basis. He got two
33   tattoos, one of Kokopelli and the other of a Grateful Dead graphic design.
34
35   Our parents would have had a fit if they had known about either the tattoos or the marijuana.
36   When George grew his hair out in college, our father didn't like it one bit. I wasn't too concerned
37   about any of this as I saw it as just a phase he was going through. I smoked marijuana and
38   have several tattoos as well, but that didn't stop me from being on the law review or getting
39   a job offer from the conservative, respected Plimpton, Standish law firm.
40
41   I encouraged George to take the time off from school and a career track. Once you start in a
42   graduate school program, the chance to take time off becomes severely limited. Though our
43   parents weren't happy about this decision, they accepted it.

1   It was only later after this lawsuit began that we found out that George was actually a few
2   credits short of his degree. He had 176 and needed 180. He never mentioned to me that he
3   had not received his diploma. I think he was a little embarrassed that he had miscalculated
4   his credits. Our parents had asked George repeatedly if he had received his degree. He told
5   them he had.
6
7   I worked for the Plimpton, Standish firm as a law clerk while attending law school. This was
8   during the same time that my brother was with Mercury Messenger, which often dispatched
9   him to law firms for document pickups. He would come by and have coffee with me when he
10 was in my building. During one of our meetings, we had discussions about the LSAT course.
11 I told him that he didn't need to take the preparatory course, that I had a book he could use
12 to study for the LSAT. He asked me for it, and I gave it to him. The LSAT is an examination you
13 have to take to get into law school, to find out where you place in law school, just like the SAT
14 was for college. When I cleaned out my brother's effects after he died, I found the book by
15 his bedside table.
16
17 My impression was that George was going to stop being a messenger by the end of the
18 summer before he was killed. Without specifying what, he had told me he had some things
19 to take care of.
20
21 He was full of questions about what I would be doing as an associate at the firm, what my
22 obligations and responsibilities were, whether or not I actually found the job interesting. I told
23 him that working as a lawyer was different than I thought it would be, far more interesting. At
24 the end of one such conversation, he laughed, put his arm around me, and said, "I see myself
25 following your path." I had to run back to work because I had a meeting, and he had a delivery.
26 But as we parted that day, it was my impression that George was interested in going forward
27 with law school.
28
29 He had all the qualities that it takes to be successful in the legal profession. But he never got
30 the chance. He knew how to write and think very well. He cared deeply for other human
31 beings; he was filled with compassion and humanity.
32
33 On June 22, 2012, I was taking my bar review class at the University of Nita. At about 4:30,
34 some friends of mine decided to go downtown to Viva Zapata's to grab a margarita. We were
35 sitting outside on the terrace. We'd only been there a few minutes, and I only had a sip or
36 two of my margarita when I heard a bunch of sirens. I don't really believe in premonitions, or
37 anything like that, but suddenly, I got really kind of shaky, really uncomfortable. I asked one of
38 my friends to take me home. On the way there, about three blocks from Memorial Hospital,
39 my cell phone rang. It was a call from my boyfriend, who said that people were trying to reach
40 me; there had been an accident and George was injured. I asked how bad it was. He said, "It's
41 bad. George is in the emergency room at Memorial Hospital."
42
43 Our parents were on an extended trip up in Alaska. They could not be reached until the next
44 day. They had to drive for ten hours to Anchorage, then get on a plane to come home. The

1 doctors did George's first brain surgery at about one o'clock in the morning. They wouldn't let
2 me stay by his bed or talk to him.
3
4 My parents got back about an hour or so after the second surgery a few days later. I could tell
5 that they were really scared. They were so distraught. They kept saying over and over to the
6 doctors, "Please do anything you possibly can so that he will live." My parents, my brother,
7 my friends, and I camped out at the hospital. We were allowed to see him the afternoon
8 following the second surgery. They had removed a portion of his skull in an attempt to relieve
9 the pressure on his brain. We could hold his hand and be in the room with him. None of us
10 wanted to stop believing that he would be okay. He didn't open his eyes or talk, but the first
11 day or two I was sure that he knew we were there. But as the days went on, he slipped away
12 from us.
13
14 After he had been there a week, the doctors and nurses told us there was total devastation
15 of his brain. He could stay on life support, but he would never wake up and he could never
16 go home. George and I had philosophical conversations about this type of thing, and I knew
17 what he would want. If he couldn't live as he had, he would not want to endure this way. And
18 so in actually saying that to the doctors, there was a sense of calmness. We knew this was the
19 decision that George would have wanted. After we walked out, my dad was trying to support
20 my mom, who was weeping. My dad started crying, too. I had heard him cry once before, and
21 it's the kind that when you hear it, it doesn't go away.

This deposition was taken in the office of defendant's counsel on April 5, 2013. The deposition
was given under oath, and was read and signed by the deponent.

Certified by:

Penelope Harrison

Penelope Harrison
Certified Shorthand Reporter
(CSR)

DEPOSITION OF SARAH PAINE
MARCH 30, 2013

1   My name is Sarah Paine. I am a trained paramedic for the Nita Fire Department. I am
2   thirty-six years old, with ten years of experience. I am single and have no children.
3
4   On June 22, 2012, I was on duty working for the Nita Fire Department as a paramedic with
5   Medic 10. At approximately 5:00 p.m., I responded to the scene of an accident at Empire Way
6   and Sunset Streets in Nita, where a bicyclist had been severely injured in a collision with a
7   vehicle. After assisting with the immediate treatment of the bicyclist, I transported him, along
8   with other medics of my unit, to Memorial Hospital.
9
10 As a trained and experienced paramedic, it was my normal practice to make a mental note
11 of any signs of the mechanism of injury at any trauma scene, noting anything that was out of
12 the ordinary. I am certain that I would have remembered anything out of the ordinary in this
13 situation with the bicyclist. This would include anything that jumped out at me at the time,
14 including the absence of a helmet.
15
16 I remembered walking past the vehicle that hit the bicyclist and seeing the indentations on
17 the windshield from the impact. If the bicyclist was not wearing a helmet at the time his
18 head hit the windshield, I would have expected big lacerations on his head. I did not see any.
19 I do not recall seeing any hair, blood, or skin embedded in or on the windshield, which is
20 consistent with the bicyclist wearing a helmet. The kind of force involved in this impact would
21 have caused the bicycle helmet to break apart.
22
23 While the report I filled out that day made no mention of a bicycle helmet being at the scene,
24 I have a recollection of either seeing a broken helmet at the scene, or hearing someone at the
25 scene make a comment about a "broken helmet."

This deposition was taken in the office of plaintiff's counsel on March 30, 2013. The deposition
was given under oath, and was read and signed by the deponent.

Certified by:

Penelope Harrison

Penelope Harrison
Certified Shorthand Reporter
(CSR)

DEPOSITION OF JAMES F. WHORL
APRIL 3, 2013

1   My name is James Whorl. I am a biomechanical engineer with a PhD in this field from
2   McGill University. I have reviewed the photos of Richard Prince's SUV; George Constantine's
3   bicycle; the police report, including accident reconstruction; and George Constantine's
4   medical records and autopsy report related to the accident. My opinions to a reasonable
5   degree of biomechanical engineering certainty are:
6
7   • The damage profile on the SUV indicates that Mr. Constantine's left side torso probably
8   hit the passenger side, and his head hit the driver side of the front windshield. This contact
9   occurred, based on police reconstruction, at between 25–36 mph. This is beyond the speed at
10   which bicycle helmets, with one to two inches of foam to absorb impact energy, are designed
11   to function.
12
13   • The contact on the windshield as well as the description of the injuries to Mr. Constantine
14   indicate that the contact with the SUV occurred on the left side of his head. Bicycle helmets
15   function best when the top of the helmet is aligned with the contact surface (as occurs when
16   thrown forward over the handlebars) and offer relatively little side protection. For reasons of
17   high speed and side contact, I feel a bicycle helmet would not have provided protection to
18   Mr. Constantine's head in this accident. There is enormous energy transfer when a speeding
19   vehicle strikes an essentially stationary human being and accelerates the individual struck
20   from zero mph to whatever speed the vehicle is traveling, all in an instant.

This deposition was taken in the office of defendant's counsel on April 3, 2013. The deposition
was given under oath, and was read and signed by the deponent.

Certified by:

Penelope Harrison

Penelope Harrison
Certified Shorthand Reporter
(CSR)

Deposition of Taylor Livingston
April 9, 2013

1   My name is Taylor Livingston. I am a certified vocational rehabilitation counselor. I have received
2   both my bachelor's degree in psychology and my master's degree in vocational rehabilitation
3   from the University of Wisconsin. I spent ten years working with injured workers in Chicago.
4   I then moved to Nita, where I have had the same basic focus. I also do vocational evaluations
5   for lawyers involved in legal cases.
6
7   I am familiar with the literature in vocational rehabilitation and attend seminars on a regular
8   basis.
9
10 I have met with the parents of George Constantine, as well as his sister and brother. I have
11 looked at his education and work history, as well as family history. As a vocational counselor,
12 once I know the strengths and weaknesses, skills and abilities of the individual, then I can look
13 to the jobs that are available in the labor force.
14
15 In this case, we are dealing with a young person, trying to figure out what he might have
16 done. Family history is one of the things that we can use as a predictor. There is literature
17 validating the relationship between family history, family attitudes, and later career success.
18
19 From my review of the records, as well as the interviews with the family, I concluded that
20 George Constantine was a person who had achieved at a very high level. He was a National
21 Merit Scholar and was eligible for an appointment to the U.S. Naval Academy, which he
22 declined. His SAT scores placed him in the ninety-sixth percentile. He graduated from high
23 school almost a year early and took college-level courses from that point on. As a National
24 Merit Scholar, he was in the top 5 percent of high school students nationally.
25
26 There was a significant emphasis on education in his family. I think that's obvious from what he
27 accomplished. His sister is currently an attorney working here in town. His brother completed
28 school and is an engineer. His father was in a position of responsibility in the airline industry.
29 Education was repeatedly stressed as an important value in this family.
30
31 Based on the record before me, the professional literature, and statistics that show that
32 86 percent of the people with his SAT scores graduate from college with a bachelor's degree and
33 62 percent of the people with his SAT score obtain an advanced degree and do postgraduate
34 work, I believe he would have completed his education, obtained an advanced degree, and
35 gone to work in a field associated with his education, which, for the most part, would have
36 been in a professional position.

This deposition was taken in the office of plaintiff's counsel on April 9, 2013. The deposition was given under oath and was read and signed by the deponent.

Certified by:

Penelope Harrison

Penelope Harrison
Certified Shorthand Reporter
(CSR)

Deposition of Richard Prince
March 15, 2013

1   My name is Richard Prince. I have been employed by Worldwide Footwear as a sales
2   representative and sales manager for the past six years. I received a bachelor's degree in
3   marketing from Indiana University.
4
5   One of our top accounts in Nita is a high-end store, Elite Fashion. I had made a sales call on
6   them on the afternoon of June 22, 2012, which lasted for several hours. I had rented the SUV
7   I was driving that day at the airport. I had a business dinner that night with a local marketing
8   consultant. We had a number of exciting promotions that were likely to increase our sales
9   dramatically. I had been to the restaurant where we were meeting once before and had a
10 general idea of where it was. I left my hotel and headed north on Empire Way. The three
11 or four intersections prior to the intersection of Empire Way and Sunset Streets had traffic
12 signals. The one at Sunset did not.
13
14 Empire Way took me through a busy tourist area, where there was a great deal of activity.
15 There were many cars and trucks in the area, as well as pedestrian traffic.
16
17 As I approached the intersection, I was traveling about 25 mph. I was watching the road and
18 paying attention to the traffic. I was scanning ahead for both cars and pedestrians.
19
20 I knew I was coming up to a crosswalk. There was pedestrian traffic on both the east and west
21 side of Empire Way. I saw a car in the left-hand southbound lane preparing to turn left. There
22 were a row of cars to my right in the other lane, trying to turn eastbound on Sunset. There
23 was heavy traffic in both lanes at this point. It was congested and somewhat backed up. I was
24 concerned that the cars to the right of me might merge into my lane, and I was reconsidering
25 trying to turn right onto Sunset Street.
26
27 I can't say where I was looking at any given point prior to the impact, but I was paying attention
28 and scanning the road ahead as I proceeded.
29
30 I really didn't know what happened when the bicyclist hit the windshield. I thought it might
31 be a foreign object that had been thrown or dropped, like a rock. I wasn't sure what it was.
32 Immediately I covered my face to protect myself because I was concerned that the bicyclist's
33 body was going to come through the windshield. After the accident, I noticed glass shards
34 throughout the interior of my car.
35
36 I took my hands down when I realized that the bicyclist wasn't going to come through the
37 windshield. Then I braked. Obviously, I was extremely concerned about what had taken place.
38 The bicyclist was breathing as he lay on the pavement, but was unconscious. He was wearing

1   what I call drab, dark clothing. He had dreadlock-type hair. He had bicycle shoes on and a
2   messenger bag that was dark in color. That's all I really remember.
3
4   It was very stressful when I gave a statement to the police later. The exact choice of words
5   I used in the statement wasn't really on my mind. I wanted to keep the content of the statement
6   basically to where my SUV was and the bicycle. I wasn't really focusing on the choice of words.
7
8   I had been texting my girlfriend on my cell phone in the minutes prior to the collision, letting
9   her know that I would be trying to catch an earlier flight. Given the heavy truck, car, and
10   pedestrian activity in the area, while my phone was still in my hand, I had stopped texting at
11   some point prior to the collision. My map and planner had not been moved from the front
12   passenger seat since I left my sales call at Elite Fashion earlier.
13
14   When the police officer questioned me at the scene about the circumstances leading up to the
15   collision, I was frightened out of my wits, completely distraught. Fearful that the officer would
16   think I had been texting immediately prior to the collision, I denied that I had been doing it at
17   all. When the officer asked to see my phone, I handed it to him without any resistance. After
18   he saw the partially completed text on the screen and asked me about it, I then admitted that
19   I had been doing this earlier.
20
21   The police officer requested that I give him a written statement. I was reluctant to do this
22   as I was in a distracted mental state. In addition, my brother-in-law is an attorney and once
23   told me that I should never volunteer any information to the police if I was to get in a traffic
24   accident.
25
26   After the office presented the statement he had written out at the scene for review and
27   signature, I crossed a number of sentences out and initialed these changes. I still was not
28   thinking clearly and refused to sign the statement.
29
30   I was not being inattentive. I was driving carefully. I have to drive frequently on business,
31   traveling to multiple states for Worldwide Footwear. I have gotten some speeding tickets over
32   the years, most of which involved no more than 10 mph over the posted limit. I did not feel
33   that I was guilty in any of these incidents, but because my work schedule is so demanding,
34   it made no sense to take time off to contest the ticket. I paid the fine because it was more
35   expedient to do so. I talked with my supervisor about this at one point, and she agreed.
36
37   I was raised in a close, nurturing family. I place a high value on human life. The fact that there
38   was a loss of life in this accident has been really difficult. I still maintain that I wasn't at fault,
39   and I couldn't have done anything differently to change the outcome. But it doesn't take away
40   from the fact that it's truly a tragedy. I feel a deep empathy for what the Constantine family
41   has gone through and will continue to go through.

This deposition was taken in the office of plaintiff's counsel on March 15, 2013. The deposition was given under oath, and was read and signed by the deponent.

Certified by:

Penelope Harrison

Penelope Harrison
Certified Shorthand Reporter
(CSR)

DEPOSITION OF GOLDIE TONE
APRIL 3, 2013

My name is Goldie Tone. I am thirty years old, married with no children. I have been a firefighter/ paramedic for five years. On June 22, 2012, I was on duty for the Nita Fire Department as a paramedic with Medic 10. My partner that day in the medical emergency vehicle was Sarah Paine. We responded to the scene of an accident at Empire Way and Sunset Streets in Nita, where a bicyclist had been hit by an SUV. When I arrived, the victim was lying on the pavement, covered with a blanket. It was obvious that he had sustained a severe head injury. While our report makes no mention of a helmet one way or the other, I do not recall ever cutting off a helmet from him. I don't remember ever seeing a helmet. I am 99 percent sure the bicyclist was not wearing one. Normally, if an injured bicyclist has a helmet, we cut it off of the person and it is retained along with any other personal property. The personal property inventory filled out by our unit on that day shows no record of a helmet.

This deposition was taken in the office of plaintiff's counsel on April 3, 2013. The deposition was given under oath, and was read and signed by the deponent.

Certified by:

Penelope Harrison

Penelope Harrison
Certified Shorthand Reporter
(CSR)

Deposition of Hughey Huff
April 7, 2013

1   My name is Hughey Huff. I own Mercury Messenger Service. I have been in the business
2   for seventeen years. My current title with the company is president and owner. George
3   Constantine worked for us as one of our bicycle messengers.
4
5   We have a computer printout of the deliveries that were performed on June 22, 2012. These
6   show the calls that came in from customers who wanted deliveries completed. They show
7   where we're picking the packages or documents up, where they're going to, and the time
8   frame that is required on the jobs.
9
10 Our company is unique in that it has a free-call system. In the normal dispatch, the calls
11 come in and the customers say when they want a delivery done. The dispatcher looks at that
12 job, and along with all the other deliveries that have to be done, assigns it to a particular
13 messenger. They will call out on the radio and say, "I want you to do this particular delivery,"
14 giving the messenger all the details.
15
16 In our free-call system, the decisions are made by all the messengers themselves. The
17 dispatcher merely calls the job out, "I have a one-hour rush job. Who wants it?" And the
18 messengers themselves claim the job if they feel they have enough time to pick up and deliver.
19
20 Like all our messengers, George Constantine was on commission. The drivers and bicyclists
21 are paid 46 percent of whatever the revenue is on the delivery. The more jobs they take, the
22 more money they make.
23
24 The last two calls to George Constantine on June 22, 2012, show a pickup at Nelson Architects
25 that was called in at 4:32 p.m., and then another one at Dimaggio & Paul, called in at 4:30
26 p.m. The first pickup was for 4:45 p.m. It was a rush that had to be delivered by 5:00 p.m.
27 We normally assume that businesses close at 5:00 p.m., unless they tell us otherwise. Since
28 George's first pickup was at 4:45, we can say with certainty that it had to be picked up and
29 delivered by either 5:00 or 5:15. The second pickup was at 5:00 p.m. and had to be delivered
30 on either a fifteen- minute or thirty-minute basis. I can't tell which by looking at the form.
31 The two pickup and delivery places were in a several-mile radius of one another in downtown
32 Nita.
33
34 We want to make sure for business purposes that deliveries occur on time, that somebody
35 isn't taking jobs that can't be accomplished reasonably. We have a system in the office, first
36 of all, that keeps the people who answer the telephone informed of what we are capable of
37 doing—and what we're not capable of doing. And we have a lighting system: when the color
38 code on the lights changes, it tells people who are answering the phone whether or not to
39 accept rushes or certain types of deliveries. Once the call comes in and the job is accepted,

1 we want to have enough people in all the right places to be able to perform that function
2 before we take the order and give it to dispatch.
3
4 Since all of our messengers are equipped with radios, they can call out to other messengers
5 if they're running short of time, and hand off a job. I don't know whether or not George
6 Constantine had any plan to hand off either of these deliveries he was assigned to do at the
7 end of the day on June 22.

This deposition was taken in the office of plaintiff's counsel on April 7, 2013. The deposition
was given under oath, and was read and signed by the deponent.

Certified by:

Penelope Harrison

Penelope Harrison
Certified Shorthand Reporter
(CSR)

DEPOSITION OF GRADY MAINE
MARCH 28, 2013

1 My name is Grady Maine. I am a professional accident reconstruction expert. I spent
2 twenty years with the Nita State Patrol. About five year into my career, I began to receive
3 specialized training in accident reconstruction. I have attended advanced courses at both the
4 Traffic Institute of Northwestern University and Texas A & M University.
5
6 I have reviewed the available information involving the bicycle/motor vehicle accident
7 between George Constantine and Richard Prince that happened in Nita on June 22, 2012.
8 Richard Prince was driving a 2012 Nissan Xterra SUV northbound on Empire Way. George
9 Constantine was riding his bicycle eastbound on Sunset Street.
10
11 My opinions are based on a review of the following information:
12
13 • The Police Traffic Collision Report.
14
15 • Copies of the Nita Police Department photographs.
16
17 • Copies of photographs of the damage to the SUV.
18
19 • Copy of the Nita police investigation file.
20
21 • Copy of the death certificate for George Constantine.
22
23 • Database information on a 2012 Nissan Xterra.
24
25 The collision occurred at 4:50 p.m. as Richard Prince was traveling northbound on Empire
26 Way, approaching the "T" intersection of Sunset Street, which is one way in the eastbound
27 direction. Mr. Constantine was working for Mercury Messengers, riding a bike westbound
28 from Sunset Street, attempting to cross Empire Way at a crosswalk. After being motioned
29 into the crosswalk by stopped southbound motorist Curtis Parsons, Mr. Constantine rode
30 westbound into the path of the northbound SUV and was struck by the front of the vehicle.
31 He died from injuries received in the collision.
32
33 Mr. Constantine entered the crosswalk at a time when Richard Prince could not have
34 avoided the collision. Even if Prince had detected Constantine at the first reasonable point of
35 perception, the collision still would have occurred and the results would have been the same.
36 The cars in the right turn lane blocked Mr. Prince's ability to see the bicyclist until it was too
37 late. I have prepared a computer animation study which demonstrates how his vision was
38 obscured by the traffic.

1   In my opinion, the speed of the SUV was approximately 25 mph based on the scene evidence
2   available. Mr. Prince told the police that he was unaware of the bicyclist until the impact. For
3   an unexpected event like this, the average perception-reaction time is 1.5 seconds. This is
4   commonly accepted and relied on by accident reconstruction experts, based on a study by
5   the University of Michigan Transportation Research Institute. I added another second to this
6   as the bicyclist was all but invisible to Mr. Prince until he began to move into the crosswalk.
7   The cars in the right turn lane blocked Mr. Prince's view when he was standing on the street
8   corner.
9
10   At 25 mph, the SUV travels approximately thirty-seven feet per second. During the 1.5-second
11   perception-reaction time following the collision, the SUV would have traveled approximately
12   fifty-five feet. The total distance from impact to rest for the SUV was about eighty-seven feet.
13   The remaining distance of thirty-two feet is the SUV has to come to a stop. It can do so in
14   thirty-two feet when traveling 25 mph with a deceleration factor of 0.65 g. Since there were
15   no skidmarks left by the SUV, this deceleration factor would be consistent with slowing rapidly
16   without leaving ABS marks.
17
18   The bicycle was carried at impact by the front of the SUV and did not begin leaving marks until
19   it was fifty-five feet from impact. This is the same distance as the reaction distance for the SUV
20   and confirms that Prince was beginning to brake as the bike came off the front of the sport
21   utility vehicle. The bike then slid for approximately forty feet until it came to a stop. When the
22   deceleration of the bike is calculated, based on the sliding distance, the post-collision speed
23   of the bike is 24.5 mph. Since the bike was accelerated to the speed of the SUV at impact, this
24   confirms the speed of the SUV at or near 25 mph.
25
26   My calculations indicate that it took the bicycle 2.2 seconds to travel 15.5 feet from its stopped
27   position of safety from the shoulder to the point of impact. The SUV was approximately
28   eighty-one feet away when the bicycle began to move from its stopped position.
29
30   In the first second of movement, the bicycle travels only three feet. That is the first reasonable
31   point of perception. Before that, there is no movement to perceive, and the bicycle is not in
32   the crosswalk. There is only three feet of movement to perceive in the first second. This means
33   that there is no reasonable opportunity to perceive until at least one second has elapsed.
34   That is the first indication that the bicyclist was going to cross, even though the SUV was close.
35
36   In the same first second, the SUV traveled approximately thirty-seven feet. It is then forty-four feet
37   away. Only 1.2 seconds remain. This is less than the average perception-reaction time. During
38   the 1.5 seconds from perception of the movement to reaction (for example, the beginning of
39   braking) the SUV would travel fifty-five feet. Even if Mr. Prince had seen Mr. Constantine at the
40   first reasonable point of perception, Mr. Prince could not have avoided the collision and the
41   impact speed still would have been 25 mph.
42
43   The findings of the Nita police detective are not entirely accurate as she assumed pre-impact
44   braking by Mr. Prince, even though he said he did not brake until after the impact. This makes
45   his speed come out higher than it really was. I have prepared a computer animation with

1   a comparable vehicle going 25 mph, which replicates all the dynamics of this collision and
2   proves that Mr. Prince's estimates of his pre-impact speed are likely accurate.
3
4   In my opinion, Mr. Constantine entered the roadway at a time when the SUV was so close that
5   Mr. Prince could not have avoided the impact. However, Mr. Constantine could have avoided
6   the collision by either not entering Empire Way when the SUV was so close as to constitute
7   an immediate hazard or by stopping his bicycle prior to reaching the point of impact. At a
8   minimum, whatever was visible to Mr. Prince was also visible to the bicyclist. The right to be
9   in a crosswalk is not absolute. A pedestrian or bicyclist may only enter the crosswalk when it is
10   safe to do so. Given that he entered the crosswalk despite the approach of the Prince vehicle,
11   it is reasonable to assume that he was being inattentive to the traffic hazards.

This deposition was taken in the office of plaintiff's counsel on March 28, 2013. The deposition was given under oath, and was read and signed by the deponent.

Certified by:

Penelope Harrison

Penelope Harrison
Certified Shorthand Reporter
(CSR)

DEPOSITION OF PATRICK RILEY, MD
APRIL 5, 2013

1　My name is Patrick Riley. I am a medical doctor with a specialty in neurology. I received
2　my undergraduate degree in biology from the University of Washington and then went on
3　to receive my medical degree at the University of Washington School of Medicine. I did
4　postgraduate training in neurology at Duke University. I currently practice as a neurologist
5　in Nita.
6
7　I was given the medical records of George Constantine, along with the police report and
8　photographs. I was asked by the attorneys for Mr. Prince to do an analysis of what difference,
9　if any, a bicycle helmet would have made in this case. I am an avid cyclist and have read about
10　and studied helmet design in that capacity. I am not a biomechanical expert.
11
12　I am relying on my personal experience as a neurologist, having treated many head injuries.
13　I am also relying on the medical records and medical literature that I have reviewed during the
14　course of my training and medical practice.
15
16　I am aware the use of bicycle helmets is not required in any state, but that it is highly advisable
17　to wear them. The head injury that George Constantine suffered when he was hit by the SUV
18　was the cause of his death.
19
20　In reviewing the medical records, I did not reach an opinion on whether or not the decedent
21　had any conscious pain and suffering between being hit and when he died. I do believe that
22　had Mr. Constantine been wearing a bicycle helmet, it would have had a substantial bearing
23　on the extent of his head injuries and markedly increased the probability of his survival. More
24　probably than not, if he had survived, he would not have had severe brain injuries if he were
25　wearing a bicycle helmet. But I would not be able to predict what type of employment he
26　would have been able to perform, had he been wearing a bicycle helmet and survived the
27　accident.

This deposition was taken in the office of plaintiff's counsel on April 5, 2013. The deposition
was given under oath, and was read and signed by the deponent.

Certified by:

Penelope Harrison

Penelope Harrison
Certified Shorthand Reporter
(CSR)

Deposition of William Gulliford
April 7, 2013

1   My name is William Gulliford. I am a forty-five-year-old certified vocational counselor. I am
2   self-employed. I have a master's degree in vocational rehabilitation counseling from the
3   University of Oregon.
4

5   I have reviewed the academic records of George Constantine, as well as his employment
6   records. I do not believe that he would have gone on to get any more than a bachelor's
7   degree, based on the available evidence and statistical abstracts of employment data.
8

9   I have relied on the Statistical Abstract of the United States, a national data book, which
10   contains virtually any statistic you would want to know about what goes on in the United States.
11   There is a big fall-off of a number of people who seek an advanced degree after getting their
12   bachelor's. Of all the people who got bachelor's degrees, four years later, only 30 percent
13   had masters degrees or the equivalent. And for doctoral degrees, it was 3 or 4 percent of the
14   initial group.
15

16   A vocational counselor has to differentiate between capacity and motivation. Mr. Constantine
17   certainly had the capacity to get an advanced degree. Capacity is like horsepower in an
18   engine or a motor. If you don't have wheels and someone to steer the car, it's not going to go
19   anywhere, even though it has a high capacity in terms of horsepower.
20

21   Motivation is difficult to measure. The only real way to do this is to examine what choices a
22   person has made and the steps that person has made to actualize these choices in life.
23

24   Mr. Constantine definitely had the capacity, but I question his motivation. All of us in life are
25   faced with forks in the road. We come to a point where we have to make a choice. What
26   I found in looking at his school and employment records was that he appears to have made
27   a fairly significant choice near the end of his last term at Nita University. He left school after
28   summer term and did not return. He did not achieve a degree. At this point, he was working
29   as a bicycle messenger, which is a nonprofessional job. He had done this for several years
30   prior to his death. There is no evidence to support the conclusion that he was headed toward
31   graduate school or a professional career.

This deposition was taken in the office of plaintiff's counsel on April 7, 2013. The deposition was given under oath, and was read and signed by the deponent.

Certified by:

Penelope Harrison

Penelope Harrison
Certified Shorthand Reporter
(CSR)

EXPERTS' REPORTS

February 15, 2013

Mr. Andrew C. Scherer
Scherer & Gillig
Nita Professional Center
Nita City, Nita

Re: Estate of George S. Constantine, deceased

Dear Mr. Scherer:

I have reviewed the information provided by your office to date concerning George Constantine, and based on this information, I have calculated the economic loss to his estate. This letter outlines the methods and assumptions used in my calculations.

In determining economic damages, I have used methodology consistent with established precedents. In wrongful death cases in which the decedent leaves no dependents, the estate of the decedent may recover for economic loss. The correct measure of damages has been determined to be a projection of future earning capacity minus the decedent's personal expenses, discounted to present value. Mr. Constantine died on June 29, 2012 at age 22.90. I relied on information published by the Insurance Commissioner's Office to determine his statistical life expectancy at the date of injury. The point of reference is the individual's age at the nearest birth date. At age 23, the statistical life expectancy for males is 50.51 years.

Work-Life Expectancy

I used Bureau of Labor Statistics Bulletin 2254, "Work-life Life Estimates: Effects of Race and Education," to determine work-life expectancy for Mr. Constantine. The information indicates that he needed an additional four credits to complete a bachelor's degree at the University of Nita. I understand that he planned to attend law school after completing his bachelor's degree. For purpose of these calculations, I assumed that he could have completed a professional degree by age 28. The work-life expectancy of a twenty-eight-year-old with fifteen or more years of education is 33.6 years. Assuming continuous labor force participation from degree completion, this implies retirement at age 61.60.

Expected Earnings

In order to project expected future earnings over work-life expectancy, it is first necessary to determine current earnings. In cases involving a young person like George Constantine, who had not yet completed his education and entered a profession, it is appropriate to use earnings data based on educational categories. As indicated above, I calculated earnings for Mr. Constantine based on the average earnings of males with professional degrees. I have assumed that, had he lived, Mr. Constantine could have had earnings comparable to the average for similarly educated males. I have relied on the census data in order to project earnings for him from age twenty-eight to the end of his statistical expectancy. It is my understanding that Mr. Constantine planned to return to college to complete his bachelor's degree, and that he was considering continuing his education in law school. The consensus category "Professional Degrees" includes individuals with degrees in law, medicine, and other professional specialty areas, and reflects the average earnings levels available to individuals working in those fields.

I have not calculated a loss to the estate for the period between the date of death and the date I assumed that Mr. Constantine would have completed his professional degree. Although he would presumably be working during that time, I assumed that the level of his earnings while he was a student, or in seasonal jobs prior to his return to school, would have only covered his living expenses during that time.

Census Data: Average Earnings by Age and Education

The U.S. Bureau of the Census current income estimates for various educational levels and ages indicate that a typical male with a professional degree can expect to earn approximately $125,290 annually. The actual annual earnings figure range from $51,529 per year for new graduates (ages 25–29) to $196,602 per year (ages 60–64).

Discounting to Present Value

Future income can be estimated by applying relevant growth trends to the base income. However, these future amounts must then be reduced to present value. This projection and reduction to present value can be combined into one step by comparing the long-term relationship of past growth trends and income with past interest rates on selected securities. Based on this comparison, I used a 1.0 percent net discount rate to determine the present value of expected earnings.

Loss to the Estate

The loss to George Constantine's estate can be measured by the difference between the present value of his projected earnings and that of his projected expenses. As a male with a professional degree, Mr. Constantine's earnings over the course of his working years would be significantly above the average for all workers in the United States. I have applied personal consumption data to the present value of the earnings projected for George Constantine to determine the present value of his future expenses. These expenses are then subtracted from projected earnings to determine the present value of economic loss to the estate. I have assumed that the pension benefits and social security payments he would have received during retirement would have covered his personal consumption during that period.

If you have any questions concerning the preceding discussion or present loss value figures, please do not hesitate to call.

Sincerely,

Roberta S. Kaylan

Roberta S. Kaylan, PhD

RSK/

ATTACHMENT A
CONCLUSIONS: PRESENT VALUE SUMMARY OF ECONOMIC LOSS TO THE ESTATE OF
GEORGE CONSTANTINE
BASED ON AVERAGE EARNINGS OF MALES WITH PROFESSIONAL DEGREES
EARNINGS, PERSONAL CONSUMPTION, AND LOSS TO THE ESTATE

EARNINGS: $3,385,168

PERSONAL CONSUMPTION: $2,200,359

LOSS TO THE ESTATE: $1,184,809

Earnings calculation begins at age twenty-eight.

Dr. Sarah J. Skinner

Financial & Economic Consultant
P.O. Box 356-B
Nita City, Nita

March 23, 2013

Teresa Brigati, Esq.
Brigati, Colombo & Hawks
500 Tower Building
Nita City, Nita

Re: <u>Constantine v. Prince</u>

Dear Ms. Brigati:

I have prepared a preliminary estimate of economic loss in this case, and it comes to $421,550. I have used the case material sent to me to arrive at this amount, and I have also analyzed Dr. Kaylan's estimate of $1,184,804.00. My methodology is similar to Dr. Kaylan's. However, there is a major difference between our approaches to the decedent's projected earnings. Whereas Dr. Kaylan assumed that Mr. Constantine would graduate from law school, I find this extremely unlikely for the following reasons:

1. Constantine had not completed his bachelor's degree from University of Nita.

2. Although he was only four credits short of the degree, he had not returned to the university for two years since his last attendance, thus demonstrating a lack of interest in finishing this law school admission requirement.

3. He had neither taken the required LSAT exam, nor registered with the LSDAS.

4. He had not applied to a law school.

5. Even if he had met the requirements above, his grade point average of 3.23 at University of Nita would have made his admission unlikely. For the 2012 entering law class at the University of Nita, only twenty-five of the 320 applicants in the 3.0–3.24 grade point average were admitted (7.8 percent success rate, and a 92.2 percent rejection rate).

6. He had left his job as a document clerk at the firm of Rosen & O'Connell soon after dropping out of the University of Nita and had become a bicycle messenger.

Although Constantine was intellectually able and a good worker, it appears that he had abandoned plans to go to law school. Therefore, I assumed Constantine would not become an attorney. However, I did assume that at some point he would finish his bachelor's degree.

Constantine was 22.90 years old on June 22, 2012, the date of the accident. (He died a week later.) His work-life expectancy (U.S. Bureau of Labor Statistics Bulletin 2254) at the time was 38.27 years. By the time of trial, 2.16 years will have elapsed, leaving 36.11 remaining years of work-life expectancy.

Annualizing his earnings at his last employer, Mercury Messenger, yields $19,821 a year. Assuming earnings of $20,000 in the next year, then rising at 3 percent a year until trial, results in past lost earnings of $43,995.

Subsequent to trial, it is assumed that he would have completed his degree and moved to a better paying position. Based on U.S. Census data for 2010 (Series P60-209), inflated by 10.2 percent to trial date, Constantine's lifetime average earnings from age twenty-five until the end of his work-life expectancy were projected at $52,152 a year. For his remaining work-life expectancy of 36.11 years, the present value of these earnings, discounted at 1 percent net, comes to $1,574,154.

It should be noted that the average earnings over his lifetime are based on median earnings data for all males with a bachelor's degree. The median is more representative of expected earnings than the average, because the latter is unduly affected by extremely high data points. The mean is 29 percent higher than the median. Actually, my calculations overstate even median earnings, reporting total money income, which includes interest, dividends and other income, rather than just earnings. Although this overstatement is of the order of 6 percent (suggesting lifetime average earnings of about $49,000 a year), it has not been factored into the calculation. Dr. Kaylan's use of (mean) data exaggerates lost earnings.

As for personal consumption, which includes social security employee contributions (not considered an income tax in Nita), 90 percent was applied to Constantine's earnings prior to trial (presumably as a bicycle messenger), and 73.5 percent on his future earnings. (As earnings rise, so does consumption, but the percentage decreases. In this case, the 90 percent consumption is $18,331 a year, while the 73.5 percent consumption is $38,332 a year.) Applying these percentages to past lost earnings yields consumption of $39,596 (90 percent × $43,995), and $1,157,003 (73.5 percent × $1,574,154) for the present value of future consumption.

In summary:

	PAST	FUTURE	TOTAL
LOST EARNINGS	$43,995	$1,574,154	$1,618,149
CONSUMPTION	$39,596	$1,157,003	$1,196,599
NET LOSS	$ 4,399	$ 417,151	$ 421,550

Thank you for the opportunity to participate in this case.

Very truly yours,

Sara J. Skinner

DR. SARAH J. SKINNER
sjs/

REPORT OF PLAINTIFF'S VOCATIONAL EXPERT, TAYLOR LIVINGSTON

As a career counselor, I look at people's backgrounds and determine what their capacities are. I have reviewed the complete educational and employment records of George Constantine. I have also interviewed his parents and both siblings extensively about his skills, goals, and aptitudes, as well as the values that existed within the culture of this family. This information allows me to render the following opinions about his career potential.

1. Had he not died in this accident, Mr. Constantine would have gone on to get a graduate degree in some field.

2. When I interviewed several close friends and his sister, all indicated that Mr. Constantine had stated a strong preference for becoming a lawyer.

3. The fact that he was taking a break from school at the time he was killed did not make Mr. Constantine less likely to return to graduate school at a later time.

4. The parents and siblings of George Constantine are successful professionals. This is a good indication of his future achievement level.

5. George Constantine tested well, was goal-oriented, and performed at a high level in school

6. Student academic performance in college is positively associated with applying, being accepted, and enrolling in graduate school.

7. George Constantine's GPA and record of doing well on standardized admission tests made him likely to get into law school.

8. The National Center for Education Statistics reports that a large majority (85 percent) of bachelor degree recipients in Mr. Constantine's age group expected to earn a graduate or professional degree.

9. Of the college graduates in this group, 83 percent of those who applied for an advanced degree were accepted and enrolled in a program.

10. There is no evidence in any of the materials I reviewed that would indicate that George Constantine used recreational drugs to an extent that would impair his earning capacity. Many successful professionals smoke marijuana with no apparent ill effects on their career.

REPORT OF DEFENDANT'S VOCATIONAL EXPERT

Vocational counselors have to make judgment calls on motivation and life direction to determine the likelihood of career success in the competitive labor market. A vocational expert in a wrongful death case of a young person who has not yet settled on a career has to look at the body of information that exists about the decedent and render opinions supported by the facts. While this undeniably is a tragic situation, sympathy must not enter into this process. My training and experience allows me to make an assessment of the future prospects of George Constantine.

1. Mr. Constantine had the intelligence to engage in a variety of occupations, including the pursuit of an advanced degree.

2. There is no indication of any definite career path in any of his academic or employment records.

3. While Mr. Constantine had the ability to pursue a law degree, it would be sheer speculation to conclude that he in fact would have gone in this direction. Mr. Constantine was four credits short of the 180 required to graduate from the University of Nita. He had no plan to complete those and had not even applied to take the LSAT.

4. Mr. Constantine's performance in college was uneven. He was able to maintain a respectable GPA only by taking a number of fairly easy classes.

5. No vocational expert can say on a more-probable-than-not basis what Mr. Constantine would have done in the future. He had been a bicycle messenger for more than two years at the time he died, which did not prepare him for any kind of professional job.

6. Even if we presume that Mr. Constantine would have gone on to law school and graduated, incomes earned by lawyers are all over the map. Some make six-figure incomes right out of school and others remain unable to get any employment in the legal profession.

7. The plaintiff's reliance on family background information to predict the future occupational success of Mr. Constantine is not valid. The fact that his sister works for a big law firm and is successful has no bearing on whether Mr. Constantine would have been able to achieve the same status.

8. Marijuana use tends to decrease one's motivation and academic performance. It is a definite possibility that this explains why Mr. Constantine seemed to have lost his prior level of ambition.

9. Mr. Constantine's alternative appearance and philosophical attitudes would have limited his vocational options.

Documents Relating to Employment Potential of Decedent

February 20, 2012

To Whom It May Concern:

During his years of study at University of Nita, it was my pleasure to have George Constantine in a number of my English courses. It was immediately clear to me that he was a student with tremendous potential. When a potentially difficult question was raised in class, I knew I could call on him for the answer. In addition to his academic prowess, he is open-minded, well-traveled, and articulate. He does not view education as something that only takes place in the confines of the classroom. He continually asked questions, probed responses, and made astute observations. He also has a great sense of humor, an attribute sometimes lacking in a student of his caliber. I view his future as very bright.

Sincerely,

George S. Ward

George S. Ward
Associate Professor
English Department
University of Nita

Student Name: George S. Constantine

Sex: Male

College/Major: Arts & Sciences

FRESHMAN YEAR
AUTUMN

SUBJECT	CREDITS	GRADE
Honors Science	5.0	2.7
Honors Western Civilization I	5.0	3.6
Sociology 101	5.0	3.3

WINTER

SUBJECT	CREDITS	GRADE
American Architecture & Urban Environment	2.0	3.6
Greek Art & Archeology	3.0	3.3
Honors Science II	5.0	2.1
Intro to Political Economics	5.0	3.3

SPRING

SUBJECT	CREDITS	GRADE
Intro to Drawing	3.0	2.8
Greek & Roman Mythology	3.0	2.3
Political Economics of Development	5.0	2.7
Rhetoric of Social & Political Movements	5.0	2.8

SOPHOMORE YEAR

AUTUMN

SUBJECT	CREDITS	GRADE
History of Western Europe	5.0	3.6
Intro to International Relations	5.0	3.0
Elementary Spanish	5.0	3.3

WINTER

SUBJECT	CREDITS	GRADE
Intro to Comparative Politics	5.0	3.2
Politics in Communication	5.0	3.4
Elementary Spanish	5.0	3.7

SPRING

SUBJECT	CREDITS	GRADE
Intro to Political Theory	5.0	3.8
American Foreign Policy	5.0	3.6
Elementary Spanish	5.0	3.4

SCHOLARSHIP STATUS: Dean's List

JUNIOR YEAR

AUTUMN

SUBJECT	CREDITS	GRADE
Intro to Theater	5.0	4.0
Western European Government	5.0	3.6
World Politics	5.0	3.6

WINTER

SUBJECT	CREDITS	GRADE
Society & Politics	5.0	3.0
Law & Society	5.0	3.5
Advanced Political Economics	5.0	3.1

SPRING

SUBJECT	CREDITS	GRADE
Contemporary American Literature	5.0	3.4
American Pop Song	5.0	4.0
Seminar, Civil Liberties	5.0	1.5

SUMMER

SUBJECT	CREDITS	GRADE
Intro to Photography	5.0	3.8
Beginning Short Story Writing	5.0	3.0

CUMULATIVE CREDIT SUMMARY

UN credits attempted: 176*

---

* 180 required for a degree

THE DHARMA MANIFESTO
By George Constantine*

We are the new dharma bums, the new Zen lunatics. I wrote this down in my journal a few days ago and today it resonated with me even more. We experience life, we live it. We are not concerned with the day-to-day maintenance of things such as jobs and "what are you going to do with yourself/who are you?" These are the unimportant questions. We occupy ourselves with questions of the now. Distractions come and go for it is nearly impossible to ignore the aspects of life that everyone deals with, and by default we must deal with them at times.

We are real, we are now, we are here. To us life is a simple series of tasks, everything can be broken down, everything can be digested in the right way, we only need to find it. We do not make things conform to us, nor do we conform to outside forces. Our existence negates the need for such attempts, we simply live.

Life is ours, not for the taking because one cannot take life, but to live. That is all we seek, to live a life of simplicity and happiness. If one can fulfill these tenets then their achievement of life has become complete, they too have joined us on the Zen pathway. In so doing will add momentum to our growing force. Like a tidal wave crashing onto the beach, we are on the curl, racing for the shoreline.

Stand from the mountain and look out upon the world and see what has become and what will become. If everyone would open their eyes, their mechanical, robot, industry-stifled, pollution-crusted, prejudice-blinded eyes to a new way, to our way. Understanding is all we ask, all we need. Remember to always live in the now, always be aware of everything and everyone.

---

* Written in his journal during his sophomore year in college.

Defendant's Employment Documents

WORLDWIDE FOOTWEAR APPLICATION FOR EMPLOYMENT

Name: *Richard E. Prince*

Home Address: *310 West 11th Street*
Anderson, IN

Position Desired: *Sales*

SSN: *231-17-6200*

Citizenship: *U.S.*

Do you have a method of transportation which will allow you to be present each working day and ontime? Yes *X* No

Is there any geographic location to which you would not be willing to relocate?
Yes_____ No _*X*_

Are you available for travel? Yes _*X*_ No_____

If hired, will you inform the company of any changes in your driving record?
Yes _*X*_ No_____

Person to be notified in case of an emergency: *Sarah Prince, mother*

Have you ever been convicted of a felony? Yes_____ No _*X*_

If yes, describe:

_____

_____

_____

Education: *High school – Anderson High School, Anderson, Indiana*

Did you graduate? *Yes*

College: *Indiana University, Bloomington*

Do you have any office skills: *n/a*

Typing Yes_____ No_____

Word processing Yes_____ No_____

Printing equipment Yes_____ No_____

Please list references:

Professor James Summerfelt
Indiana University
Bloomington, Indiana

Dan K. Fisher
225 Edgewood Drive
Anderson, M

James C. Werbe
26 Country Club Drive
Anderson, M

APPLICANT'S CERTIFICATION AND AGREEMENT

I hereby certify that the answers given and the statements made are true and correct and that any misrepresentation by me in this application will be sufficient cause for cancellation of this application and for termination from the service of the Corporation. I hereby authorize all my previous employers or references to furnish any information concerning my background, as well as for the Department of Motor Vehicles to furnish all information about my driving record.

Richard E. Prince

Applicant's Signature

9/20/2006

Date

WORLDWIDE FOOTWEAR

PERFORMANCE EVALUATION OF

RICHARD E. PRINCE

Date: 12/22/2011

Richard has proven to be a consistent high-volume sales producer. He puts in a great deal of effort and gets excellent results.

However, his lack of interpersonal skills continues to be a weak spot. Richard's single-minded focus on his career advancement has caused resentment by his co-workers. He is not seen as a team player. Over the years, he has improved in this area for short periods, only to return to old habits.

He must strive for greater empathy, taking the time to see things from the perspective of others rather than focusing only on his own needs. Richard also should tone down his superior attitude, allowing co-workers to express their thoughts. He understands that this continues to be area of weakness and will try to correct it in the future.

Jeffrey Hawks

Jeffrey Hawks
Director, Human Resources
Worldwide Footwear

RULES FOR DRIVERS OF COMPANY VEHICLES

SCOPE

This policy applies to all drivers of company vehicles and all divisions. It supersedes all previous policies and practices on the subject.

I. PURPOSE

To establish fair and clear policies for drivers of company vehicles in order to reduce costs and limit liability and assure continued insurance coverage.

II. ADMINISTRATIVE PROCEDURES

a. In order to be in compliance with the OSHA Motor Vehicle Standard 55-FR-28728, it is Worldwide Footwear's policy to require all employees to wear seat belts while operating or riding in company-owned or leased vehicles, or in other vehicles while on company business.

b. It is the responsibility of the employees who drive company vehicles to maintain appropriate operating licenses. It is also their responsibility to provide Worldwide Footwear the information that may impact their continued authorization to drive (moving violations, restricted licenses, suspensions, etc.). States that issue such licenses and insurance companies do not distinguish between driving records of people who drive for company business or personal use. Therefore, an employee's total driving record is the basis for insurance company coverage and potential future legal liability questions. As a result, anyone who drives a company vehicle must report any moving violation that he or she receives regardless of whether it was personal or company business.

c. Upon full review of the circumstances, the following offenses could result in Worldwide Footwear not allowing the employee to continue to drive on company business. If the removal of this privilege results in the employee no longer being able to perform their job responsibilities effectively and it is determined that other positions in the company are not available, these violations could result in discharge from the company. A full review of these circumstances will be conducted by the Director of Insurance and Risk Management and the Vice President of Human Resources, and will also involve the input of the respective division management.

Further, for

1. Conviction for driving under the influence or while intoxicated and/or impaired—first offense.

2. Conviction for reckless driving—first offense.

3. Conviction of a felony with the vehicle—first offense.

4. Conviction for fleeing an officer—first offense.

5. The accumulation of more than half the points at which the licensing state would suspend the individual driver's license.

d. Failure to notify Worldwide Footwear of any moving violations or other matters related to driving record will be subject to Worldwide Footwear immediately revoking the privilege to drive company vehicles.

I hereby acknowledge receipt of Worldwide Footwear's policy, "Rules For Drivers of Company Vehicles."

Richard E. Prince

Applicant's Signature

9/20/2006
Date

ABSTRACT OF DRIVING RECORD
RICHARD E. PRINCE

DATE	VIOLATION	DISPOSITION
5/15/2010	Speeding. 55 mph in a 30 mph zone	Paid fine without admitting guilt.
10/22/2010	Doing 75 mph in a 70 mph zone	Paid fine without admitting guilt.
4/16/2011	Speeding. 45 mph in a 35 mph zone	Paid fine without admitting guilt.
12/18/2011	Speeding. 45 mph in a 35 mph zone	Paid fine without admitting guilt.

MUNICIPAL COURT OF NITA DOCKET

CITY OF NITA,   )

)   Case No. 2361239

Plaintiff   )

)   CHARGES

v.   )

)

RICHARD E. PRINCE,   )

)

Defendant.   )

)

Violation Date:	6/22/2012
Negligent driving.	Second degree.
Disposition:	Nolo Contendre. Forfeited bail. Case closed.

LEARNED TREATISES

Thoughts on Preventing Negligent Hiring and Supervision Claims for Employees Who Drive on the Job

By: Will B. Good, PhD, *Risk Management News*, August 2011

Any company faces significant risks when its employees drive company vehicles, or even rental vehicles, while they are in the course of employment. If a company has an open position which requires any driving of a company vehicle, it is recommended that the applicant's driving record be checked. It is extremely important for any company that hires people to drive company vehicles to inquire into past driving performance. Driving records can reveal a pattern of reckless behavior and can effectively be used as a periodic review for current employees.

A driver's license record check will generally show violations for the past three years. It is important to obtain fresh history of this on a regular basis.

LEARNED TREATISE SYNOPSIS—ACCIDENT RECONSTRUCTION

Louis R. Charles, *Accident Reconstruction Principles*

Perception-response time begins when an object or condition for concern enters the driver's visual field and the first step concludes when the driver develops a conscious awareness that something is present.

Using an appropriate driver reaction time in accident avoidance maneuvers is of critical importance. This is an area where experts frequently move to the extreme corners of the range to prove their point and support their opinion. The reaction times under normal conditions in accident avoidance braking maneuvers range from 1 second to 1.5 seconds.

Given a reasonably clear stimulus and a straightforward situation, there are good data indicating that most drivers, i.e., 85–95 percent, will respond by about 1.5 seconds after the first appearance of the object or condition of concern.

The evidence also indicates that the minimum perception-response time for this straightforward situation is about 0.75 seconds. Thus, the probable range of perception response times for reasonably straightforward situations should be 0.75 to about 1.5 seconds. Please note these values are not chiseled in stone on tablets along with other commandments.

The normal acceleration rate of a passenger car going from zero to less than 20 mph is forty-eight feet per second.

Published studies of the average male or female bicyclist acceleration rate, on an average ten-speed-type bicycle, show that the bicyclist can go from a stop to a distance of forty feet in about 3.3 seconds.

Jury Instructions

NITA
GENERAL JURY INSTRUCTIONS[1]

The following jury instructions are intended for use with any of the files contained in these materials regardless of whether the trial is in Nita state court or in federal court. In addition, each of the files contains special instructions dealing with the law applicable in the particular case. The instructions set forth here state general principles that may be applicable in any of the cases and may be used at the discretion of the trial judge.

PART I
PRELIMINARY INSTRUCTIONS GIVEN PRIOR TO THE EVIDENCE
(FOR CIVIL OR CRIMINAL CASES)

NITA INSTRUCTION 01:01—INTRODUCTION

You have been selected as jurors and have taken an oath to well and truly try this cause. This trial will last one day.

During the progress of the trial there will be periods of time when the Court recesses. During those periods of time, you must not talk about this case among yourselves or with anyone else.

During the trial, do not talk to any of the parties, their lawyers, or any of the witnesses.

If any attempt is made by anyone to talk to you concerning the matters here under consideration, you should immediately report that fact to the Court.

You should keep an open mind. You should not form or express an opinion during the trial and should reach no conclusion in this case until you have heard all of the evidence, the arguments of counsel, and the final instructions as to the law that will be given to you by the Court.

NITA INSTRUCTION 01:02—CONDUCT OF THE TRIAL

First, the attorneys will have an opportunity to make opening statements. These statements are not evidence and should be considered only as a preview of what the attorneys expect the evidence will be.

Following the opening statements, witnesses will be called to testify. They will be placed under oath and questioned by the attorneys. Documents and other tangible exhibits may also be received as evidence.

---

1. The instructions contained in this section are borrowed or adapted from a number of sources including California, Illinois, Indiana, Washington, and Colorado pattern jury instructions.

If an exhibit is given to you to examine, you should examine it carefully, individually, and without any comment.

It is counsel's right and duty to object when testimony or other evidence is being offered that he or she believes is not admissible.

When the Court sustains an objection to a question, the jurors must disregard the question and the answer, if one has been given, and draw no inference from the question or answer or speculate as to what the witness would have said if permitted to answer. Jurors must also disregard evidence stricken from the record.

When the Court sustains an objection to any evidence, the jurors must disregard that evidence.

When the Court overrules an objection to any evidence, the jurors must not give that evidence any more weight than if the objection had not been made.

When the evidence is completed, the attorneys will make final statements. These final statements are not evidence, but are given to assist you in evaluating the evidence. The attorneys are also permitted to argue in an attempt to persuade you to a particular verdict. You may accept or reject those arguments as you see fit.

Finally, just before you retire to consider your verdict, I will give you further instructions on the law that applies to this case.

PART II
FINAL INSTRUCTIONS
GENERAL PRINCIPLES
GENERAL INSTRUCTIONS FOR BOTH CIVIL AND CRIMINAL CASES

NITA INSTRUCTION 1:01—INTRODUCTION

Members of the jury, the evidence and arguments in this case have been completed, and I will now instruct you as to the law.

The law applicable to this case is stated in these instructions, and it is your duty to follow all of them. You must not single out certain instructions and disregard others.

NITA INSTRUCTION 1:04—EXPERT WITNESSES

You have heard evidence in this case from witnesses who testified as experts. The law allows experts to express an opinion on subjects involving their special knowledge, training and skill, experience, or research. While their opinions are allowed to be given, it is entirely within the province of the jury to determine what weight shall be given their testimony. Jurors are not bound by the testimony of experts; their testimony is to be weighed as that of any other witness.

NITA INSTRUCTION 1:05—DIRECT AND CIRCUMSTANTIAL EVIDENCE

The law recognizes two kinds of evidence: direct and circumstantial. Direct evidence proves a fact directly; that is, the evidence by itself, if true, establishes the fact. Circumstantial evidence is the proof of facts or circumstances that give rise to a reasonable inference of other facts; that is, circumstantial evidence proves a fact indirectly in that it follows from other facts or circumstances according to common experience and observations in life. An eyewitness is a common example of direct evidence, while human footprints are circumstantial evidence that a person was present.

The law makes no distinction between direct and circumstantial evidence as to the degree or amount of proof required, and each should be considered according to whatever weight or value it may have. All of the evidence should be considered and evaluated by you in arriving at your verdict.

NITA INSTRUCTION 1:06—CONCLUDING INSTRUCTION

The Court did not in any way and does not by these instructions give nor intimate any opinions as to what has or has not been proven in the case, or as to what are or are not the facts of the case.

None of these instructions states all of the law applicable, but all of them must be taken, read, and considered together as they are connected with and related to each other as a whole.

You must not be concerned with the wisdom of any rule of law. Regardless of any opinions you may have as to what the law ought to be, it would be a violation of your sworn duty to base a verdict upon any other view of the law than that given in the instructions of the court.

GENERAL INSTRUCTIONS FOR CIVIL CASES
NITA INSTRUCTION 2:01—BURDEN OF PROOF

When I say that a party has the burden of proof on any issue, or use the expression "if you find," "if you decide," or "by a preponderance of the evidence," I mean that you must be persuaded from a consideration of all the evidence in the case that the issue in question is more probably true than not true.

Any findings of fact you make must be based on probabilities, not possibilities. If may not be based on surmise, speculation, or conjecture.

SPECIFIC INSTRUCTIONS FOR THIS CASE

NITA INSTRUCTION 3:01— CLAIMS OF PARTIES

The plaintiff claims that the defendant was negligent because he was distracted by text messaging, failed to yield the right of way to a bicyclist in a crosswalk, failed to keep a proper lookout, and drove at an excessive speed for conditions. The plaintiff claims that the defendant's conduct was a proximate cause of injuries and damage to the decedent. The defendant denies these claims.

The defendant claims that the decedent was negligent in leaving the shoulder or other place of safety and moving into the path of his vehicle when Prince was so close that it was impossible for him to stop, and in failing to see and avoid the defendant's vehicle. The defendant claims this was a proximate cause of decedent's death and plaintiff's damages. The plaintiff denies these claims.

The defendant further denies the nature and extent of the claimed damages.

NITA INSTRUCTION 3:02—BURDEN OF PROOF

The plaintiff has the burden of proving each of the following propositions:

First, that the defendant acted, or failed to act, in one of the ways claimed by the plaintiff and that in so acting, or failing to act, the defendant was negligent;

Second, that the negligence of the defendant was a proximate cause of the death of George Constantine;

Third, that the death of George Constantine caused plaintiff damages.

If you find from your consideration of all the evidence that each of these propositions has been proved against the defendant, your verdict should be for the plaintiff and against the defendant. On the other hand, if any of these propositions has not been proved against the defendant, your verdict should be for the defendant.

Defendant Prince has the burden of proving both of the following propositions:

First, that the decedent, George Constantine, acted, or failed to act, in one of the ways claimed by the defendant, and that in so acting or failing to act, the decedent was negligent;

Second, that the negligence of the decedent was a proximate cause of the plaintiff's damages and was therefore contributory negligence.

NITA INSTRUCTION 3:03—NEGLIGENCE

Negligence is the failure to exercise ordinary care. It is the doing of some act that a reasonably careful person would not do under the same or similar circumstances or the failure to do something that a reasonably careful person would have done under the same or similar circumstances.

Ordinary care means the care a reasonably careful person would exercise under the same or similar circumstances.

NITA INSTRUCTION 3:04—CONTRIBUTORY NEGLIGENCE

Contributory negligence is negligence on the part of the decedent that is a proximate cause of the injury complained of. If you find contributory negligence, you must determine the degree of negligence, expressed as a percentage, attributable to the decedent. The court will furnish you a special verdict form for this purpose. Your answers to the questions in the special verdict form will furnish the basis by which the court will reduce the amount of any damages you find to have been sustained by the plaintiffs, by the percentage of such contributory negligence.

NITA INSTRUCTION 3:05—STATUTORY VIOLATION

The violation, if any, of a statute is not necessarily negligence, but may be considered by you as evidence in determining negligence.

NITA INSTRUCTION 3:06—STATUTE FOR CROSSWALK DUTY OF CARE

At the time of the occurrence, a statute provided as follows:

When traffic control signals are not in place, the operator of an approaching vehicle shall stop to allow a pedestrian using an unmarked or marked crosswalk, to cross the roadway when the pedestrian is upon the half of the roadway upon which the vehicle is traveling.

A person operating a bicycle across a roadway upon and along a crosswalk shall have all the rights and duties applicable to a pedestrian under the same circumstances, but shall yield to pedestrians upon and along a crosswalk. No person operating a bicycle shall suddenly enter a crosswalk into the path of a vehicle which is so close that the driver cannot yield safely.

NITA INSTRUCTION 3:07—GENERAL DUTY OF CARE

Every person has a duty to see what would be seen by a person exercising ordinary care.

It is the duty of every person using a public street or highway, whether a pedestrian or a driver of a vehicle, to exercise ordinary care to avoid placing himself or others in danger and to exercise ordinary care to avoid a collision.

Every person using a public street or highway has the right to assume that other persons thereon will use ordinary care and will obey the rules of the road, and has a right to proceed on such assumption until he knows, or in the exercise of ordinary care should know, to the contrary.

NITA INSTRUCTION 3:08—MORTALITY TABLES

According to mortality tables, the average life expectancy of a man aged twenty-two years is 51.43 years. This one factor is not controlling, but should be considered in connection with all the other evidence bearing on the same question, such as that pertaining to the health, habits, and activity of the person whose life expectancy is in question.

IN THE SUPERIOR COURT OF THE STATE OF NITA
FOR DARROW COUNTY

MELINA CONSTANTINE, as)
Personal Representative of)
the Estate of GEORGE)
CONSTANTINE,)
) SPECIAL VERDICT FORM
Plaintiff,)
)
v.)
)
RICHARD PRINCE,)
Defendant.)
_____)

We, the jury, make the following answers to the questions submitted by the court:

QUESTION NO. 1: Was the defendant negligent?

ANSWER: _____ YES _____ NO

If you answer Question No. 1 "no," sign and return this verdict. If you answer Question No. 1 "yes," then answer Question No. 2.

QUESTION NO. 2: Was such negligence a proximate cause of damage to plaintiff?

ANSWER: _____ YES _____ NO

If you answer Question No. 2 "no," sign and return this verdict. If you answer Question No. 2 "yes," then answer Question No. 3.

QUESTION NO. 3: What do you find to be the estate's amount of damages?

Economic Loss to the Estate of George Constantine

ANSWER: $_____

QUESTION NO. 4: Was decedent George Constantine also negligent?

ANSWER: _____ YES _____ NO

If you answer Question No. 4 "no," skip Question No. 5 and answer Question No. 6. If you answer Question No. 4 "yes," answer Question No. 5.

QUESTION NO. 5: Was decedent's negligence a proximate cause of plaintiffs' damages?

ANSWER: _____ YES _____ NO

If you answer Question No. 5 "yes," answer Question No. 6.

QUESTION NO. 6:   Assume that 100 percent represents the total combined fault that proximately caused the plaintiffs damages. What percentage of this 100 percent is attributable to the decedent's negligence and what percentage of this 100 percent is attributable to the defendant. (Your total must equal 100 percent.)

ANSWER: PERCENTAGE

To decedent George Constantine   _____%

To defendant Richard Prince   _____%

                                        TOTAL 100%

Sign and return this verdict.

DATED: _____   _____

                                        FOREPERSON

EXHIBITS

Exhibit 1

Police Diagram

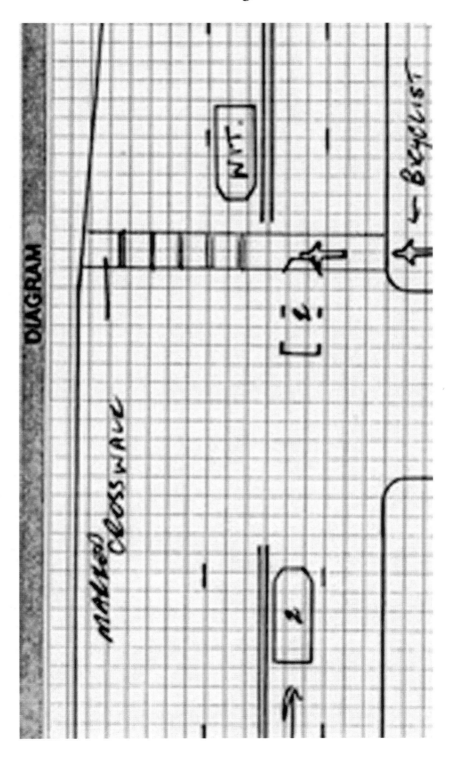

Exhibit 2

Crosswalk Looking South

Exhibit 3

Crosswalk Looking West

Exhibit 4

Heading North, Approaching the Crosswalk

Exhibit 5

Available View with Car in Right Lane

Exhibit 6

Pedestrian Sign

Exhibit 7

Bicyclist at Point of Impact

Exhibit 8

Bicycle on Street

Exhibit 9

Blood Smear on Street

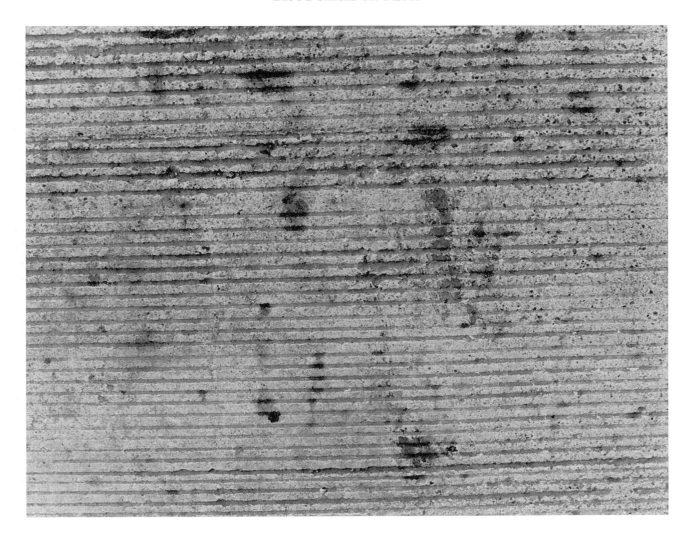

Exhibit 10

Distance Shot—Bicycle, Body, and SUV

Exhibit 11

Orange Cone Showing Point of Impact

Exhibit 12

SUV—Dent above Right Headlight (1)

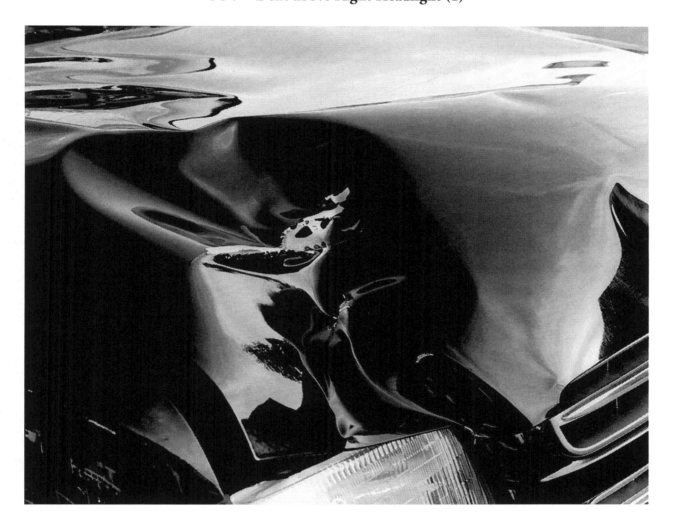

Exhibit 13

SUV—Dent above Right Headlight (2)

Exhibit 14

SUV—Headlight

Exhibit 15

SUV—Front Passenger Side

Exhibit 16

SUV—Right Front View

Exhibit 17

SUV—Windshield Close-up

Exhibit 18

SUV—Stopping Point after Impact

Exhibit 19

Bicycle by Curb

Exhibit 20

Bicycle against SUV

Exhibit 21

Defense Animation Still 1

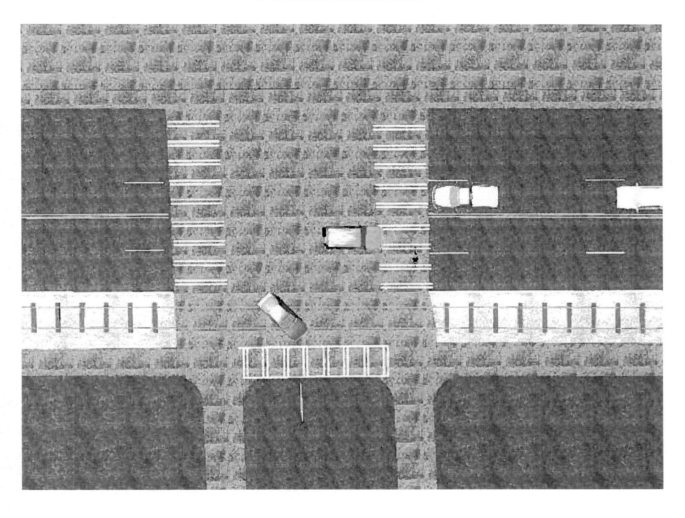

Exhibit 22

Defense Animation Still 2

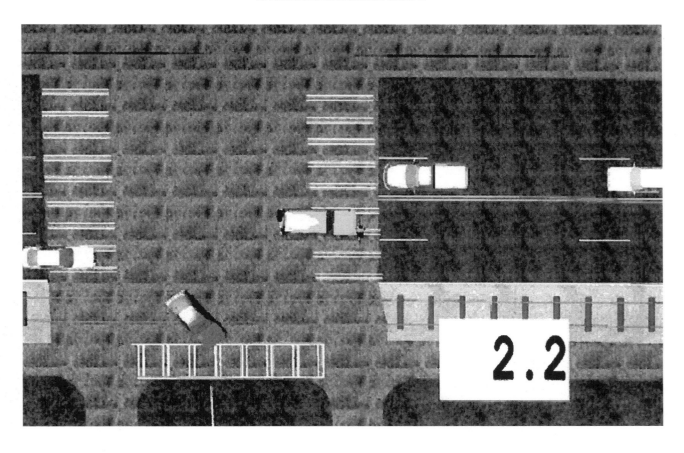

Exhibit 23

Animation Still—Driver's View One Block before Impact

Exhibit 24

Animation Still—Driver's View at Impact

Exhibit 25

Animation Still—Overview

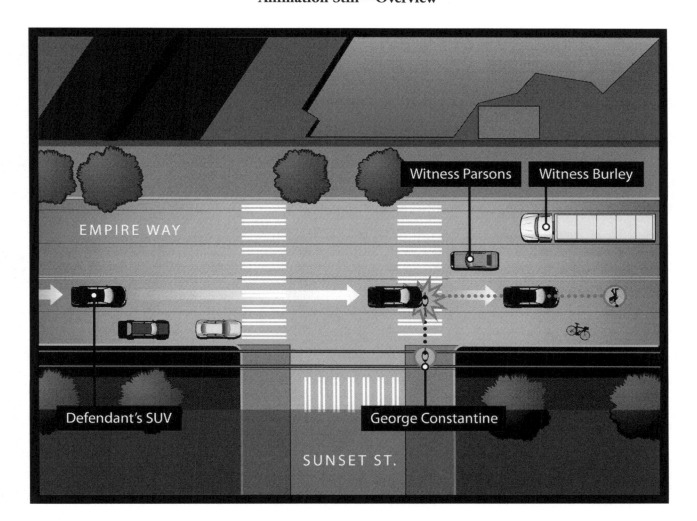

Exhibit 26

Animation Still—North View

Exhibit 27

Animation Still—South View

Exhibit 28

Animation Still—Impact, East View

Made in the USA
Las Vegas, NV
26 December 2021